Mud in Your Eye

Mud in Your Eye

Gord Penner

MUD IN YOUR EYE
Copyright © 2009 Gordon Penner

ISBN-10: 1-897373-96-1
ISNB-13: 978-1-897373-96-5

Printed by Word Alive Press

WORD ALIVE PRESS
Just Write!

131 Cordite Road, Winnipeg, Manitoba, R3W 1S1
www.wordalivepress.ca

Printed in Canada.

DEDICATION

To my mom—

*Thank you for your love and guidance,
your prayers, and the example you set forth
as you trusted God when all seemed impossible.*

ACKNOWLEDGEMENTS

Thank you, Jack and Elsie, Jerry & Audrey for your love, patience and teaching. You sowed good seed in my life and it has not come back void (Isaiah 55: 10–11 NIV).

CONTENTS

INTRODUCTION

Living the Christian life can be difficult—in fact, it is actually impossible to live it out in our own strength.

Although we readily give mental assent to this, our lives betray that we feel that we are able to accomplish some of the smaller tasks in our lives without God's help and direction. But God is not only concerned about the big things in our lives but the small things as well.

We've all heard that before. And yet, it is possible, the more often we hear these statements, to become numb, even "blind," to the truth they communicate.

This book, *Mud in Your Eye*, is an attempt to aid you in seeing God and his Word from an angle that you may have never considered looking at. My desire and hope is that the pages following will create a thirst in you for God and his Word.

As you wash the mud from your eyes, that is, as you remove the things that keep you from seeing God for who he really is, I pray that new insights into his great love and compassion for you would equip you in understanding your right standing in Jesus Christ.

May grace, peace, joy and love fill you now and in the days to follow as you grow in God's grace.

~Gord

Mud in Your Eye
(Part One)

As he went along, he saw a man blind from birth. ~JOHN 9:1

After answering the question from his disciples as to who was to blame for the man's blindness, Jesus spit in the dirt to make mud, put it in the man's eyes and told him to go wash it off in a pool called "Siloam." So the man went to the pool, washed off the mud, and came back with full sight—he could see for the first time in his life.

The religious leaders were doubtful of what went on, so they questioned both the man and his parents. They seemed reluctant to accept what happened, much less believe it.

Therefore the Pharisees also asked him how he had received his sight. "He put mud on my eyes," the man replied, "and I washed, and now I see." ~JOHN 9:15

Which brings me to the title of this book.

I have never experienced physical blindness, but there have been many situations and circumstances where I have needed to see beyond what I could see, to get past my limited sight (or "in-sight") and allow Jesus to correct or even completely open up my interpretation of what was going on around me.

We need Jesus' to help us see. And we gain that help through his Word (the Bible), his Holy Spirit (who he has given to all who accept him as their Lord & Saviour), and even teachers and preachers. That's what this book is all about: helping you "see" (understand) that God's Word is the answer to any question, any problem, any situation.

> *For the Word of God is living and active. Sharper than any double-edged sword, it penetrates even to dividing soul and spirit, joints and marrow; it judges the thoughts and attitudes of the heart.* ~HEBREWS 4:12

Maybe you have looked into the Bible and just didn't know where to start. Maybe you feel that you are too far gone or too hopeless or any other excuse the devil would like you to believe about your situation. Let me tell you, God's love for you is so massive that he sent his one and only Son, Jesus Christ, to die on a cross to pay for your sins.

> *For God so loved the world that he gave his one and only Son, that whoever believes in him shall not perish but have eternal life.* ~JOHN 3:16

God knows exactly where you are at. He is completely aware of what is going on in your life. But then, you may ask, "Why on earth is all this bad stuff happening to me?"

> *A man's own folly ruins his life, yet his heart rages against the Lord.* ~PROVERBS 19:3

> *He who walks with the wise grows wise, but a companion of fools suffers harm.* ~PROVERBS 13:20

Much of the "stuff" that goes on in our lives is self-inflicted; we bring it on ourselves by ignoring good council and making poor choices. However, God never created anyone to be a victim. He created us in his own image (Genesis1:27) and created each one of us with a plan. And that plan is a great one.

"For I know the plans I have for you," declares the Lord, "plans to prosper you and not to harm you, plans to give you hope and a future." ~JEREMIAH 29:11

If you want to learn more, keep on reading. This book is a teaching tool to encourage you—not just a quick devotional for the day but a challenge to get closer to God in prayer, in study, in trust and in service.

I pray that the eyes of your heart may be opened so that you will know the hope to which Jesus has called you, the riches of his glorious inheritance in the saints, and his incomparably great power for us who believe. I bless you in Jesus' name.

Mud in Your Eye (Part Two)

John 9:1-41

So back to that blind guy...

I have been thinking more about that situation, and the more I think about it, the more questions come to mind.

First of all, the guy was blind, not deaf, so he could hear what was going on around him. I wonder if he was ever mocked for being blind, or if maybe he was often the centre of cruel jokes and tricks. I wonder what it is like to be blind and have your coming and going dependent on someone feeling like they have the time to help you out. I wonder what it is like to be led around by the hand to places familiar and unfamiliar, hearing voices without faces, being within earshot of laughter without knowing if it's directed at you or even just enduring rude remarks.

Now there he was, in the centre of a group. He could hear people talking: "Jesus, who's fault is it that this man is born blind?" Maybe it was just a question. But I wonder what if felt like for the blind man to hear that, to consider that possibly it was because he was under God's wrath that he was born blind.

Then Jesus spit into the dirt to make mud.

Have you ever stopped to consider how much spit it would take to turn dry dirt into mud? I don't think this all took place in the span of 30 seconds; it must have taken some time. Did a crowd gather to watch the spectacle? Where there other remarks from those who were there?

Then, when the mud is ready, Jesus put it on the blind man's eyes. Again, I have to wonder what this guy was thinking. Was this a cruel joke … was he being mocked?

Jesus told him to go wash in the pool.

If we are not careful, we can approach reading God's Word as merely mechanically processing through words on a page, when in reality, we are on the very threshold of engaging with THE living Word. Often we don't stop long enough to really think through what is being said, and maybe even more tragically, we miss what is being taught.

Have you been having a tough time "seeing" in the situation you are currently in because you are blind to the spiritual help that is standing right in front of you? Are you willing to have mud smeared on your eyes? Do you trust Jesus enough—do you want to see badly enough—that you're willing to let Jesus have his way in your life, no matter how it looks?

Too many times we try to operate by our own rules, based on the way we feel our lives should go. In reality, we are saying, "God I don't trust you. I don't think you can do better with my life than I can."

Just reading that makes me feel weak in the knees!

When we try doing life our own way, not God's way, we end up taking on responsibility for something we were not intended for in the first place. That is not to say that we are to just sit back and do nothing because God is in control—it means that we need to turn our full trust over to his care, to his directions. That is when we begin to see.

The blind guy was sent over to the pool to wash the mud off his eyes and face. Trusting God means you do whatever he says, whether you understand the reasoning behind it or not. That kind of obedience honours God. Are you willing to obey? To step out and do something that you know you should do but are just too afraid of what others will think?

That's the question each one of us has to answer for ourselves. Is stepping out and living your life for Jesus the step of obedience that you know you're being called to?

Perhaps the blind man knew, as Jesus put the mud on his eyes, that he would be healed and would be able to see again. But I doubt he anticipated that he'd be asked to walk away (in faith) to "see" the miracle come to pass. Jesus told him to "go wash in the pool." What was the guy feeling and thinking as he heard the voices fade behind him as he was led away to the pool? "Is this for real? What if this doesn't work? Wait—what if it DOES work? How will I recognize anybody?"

You may well have had times in your life, maybe even right now, when it feels like God's power is gone from your life or that you have walked too far away. Listen to Jesus telling you, "Wash in the pool." Get into God's Word again (or for the first time). The Word will rinse out of your eyes whatever it is that is blocking you from seeing Jesus.

The door we are most afraid to open and go through may be the very one that leads to the place where we will meet God in a powerful way.

If you don't know Jesus as your personal Lord and Saviour and have never personally asked him to come into your life, right now you have the opportunity to do that.

Everyone who calls on the name of the Lord will be saved. ~ACTS 2:21

If you have not yet asked Jesus Christ to be your Lord and Saviour, you can do that right now. This prayer is so powerful that if you pray it and you mean it, saying these words from your heart will give you a whole new start with God, a clean slate. That doesn't mean you will be able to sit back and let God do all the things that you need to clean up in your life. What it does mean is that you will now have access to eternal power that will give you the wisdom and insight you will need to walk in the path of life.

"God I'm sorry for the way I have lived my life. Forgive me, clean me up; I want Jesus to be my Lord and Saviour. Help me to live for you, from this day forward I choose to serve you. Thank you for your forgiveness and for setting me free through Jesus, my Saviour. In His name I pray—Amen."

If you just prayed that, and meant it, your name has been written down in God's book of life. You are a born-again child of God. CONGRATULATIONS! Now, you need to get into God's Word, and that may take some help from others who know it better than you do right now. Find a good Bible-believing church that teaches the Word of God.

Chocolate, Rabbits and Eggs

Easter has nothing to do with chocolate, eggs or rabbits. As time has gone on, chocolate helicopters, flowers, cars and hero figures are almost out-numbering the rabbits. It's more about selling chocolate than any part of the real reason for celebration.

Chocolate wars aside, however, Easter has everything to do with every day of our lives!

Allow me to give you a brief history lesson. God created the world (Genesis 1:1). He created mankind (vv. 26–27), then gave them rule over the earth (v. 28). The devil, who disguised himself as a serpent, deceived Eve and Adam into going against what God had told Adam not to do (3:1). They went against God's command, listening to the lies of the devil, and the devil usurped the rule they had over the world.

> The god of this age has blinded the minds of unbelievers, so that they cannot see the light of the gospel of the glory of Christ, who is the image of God. ~2 CORINTHIANS 4:4

The devil only comes to steal, kill and destroy, but Jesus has come to give us life and life to the full (John

10:10). We are all born into a sinful world and we have all sinned (Romans 3:23). Without Jesus, we are doomed to live under the control of the devil, lost in sin on the road to hell.

Now this is what Easter is all about. Because we can't do anything about our sin and because God's love for people is so massive, he sent Jesus to get back the power of death that the devil had hung on to for so long and to get back that which was lost in the Garden of Eden through Adam and Eve (John 3:16).

God gave power and authority to man, and it was taken away from man by the devil, therefore a man had to come and take back what the devil stole to begin with. So Jesus came into this world as a baby (that's the story of Christmas), grew up and at 33 years old was tortured, mocked and killed by being nailed to a cross.

The Bible says,

For the wages of sin is death, but the gift of God is eternal life in Christ Jesus our Lord. ~ROMANS 6:23

Jesus took what we owed—the punishment for our sins (past, present and future)—and paid for it by his death. And not only that, he came back to life (John 20:15, 26; 21:1). Jesus went back to heaven and is going to come back to take all those who call him Lord and Saviour to be with him for eternity.

Today the battle still rages between good and evil. Popular bands and movies mock at the idea. Movies like to make it look like the dark side is all-powerful and victorious and that angels freak out when demons come around, but nothing could be further from the truth. God alone is all-powerful. The devil will get what's coming to him.

I know that's a whirlwind tour of the Bible, but the point is Easter is about the love of God for his people, a love so massive that he's not willing that any should die (2 Peter 3:9). God sent Jesus, his only Son, to take the sins of the world upon himself and become sin for us (2 Corinthians 5:21). We would get his righteousness and he would get our sin and punishment, which was death.

But now look at this verse. Jesus is alive!

I am the Living One; I was dead, and behold I am alive for ever and ever! And I hold the keys of death and Hades. ~REVELATION 1:18

Death no longer has to rule in your life. You no longer have to live your life in fear and shame and hopelessness. Jesus has come to bring you life—great life, powerful life. All you need to do to receive that life is call on him.

Under What Conditions?

We live in a world of conditions. We have to complete all our high school courses with a satisfactory mark or we don't graduate. We have to graduate in order to obtain a certificate. We have to be a certain age to obtain a driver's license to legally operate a motor vehicle. If we don't have the money we can't by the house, the car, etc. If we meet the conditions, all is well—but if we choose instead to make up our own rules, look out! The conditions exist for a purpose.

Of course, this is all quite obvious. Or is it?

How often do we expect to be blessed "just because" when, for the most part, we are not meeting or even seeking to learn the conditions? When blessing does not seem to be coming our way we start looking in all the wrong places and asking all the wrong questions.

What did I do? Is God mad at me? Has God turned his back on me?

Perhaps we have forgotten that God has outlined conditions for us in his Word. For instance, a person can only be saved by accepting the free gift Jesus offers (John14:6; Acts 4:12). You have to meet the condition— invite Jesus into your heart (life) and accept his Lordship—

then you receive salvation (Romans 10:9–10). "But I want to do things my way!" doesn't even factor into the equation. Interacting with God's Word isn't like going to a grocery store to pick and choose what you want when you want it. It is more like a train needing tracks to keep it moving in the way it was designed to. Some see God's Word as a list of dos and don'ts, but in reality, his Word sets out the "tracks" to get us to the place where he knows we will prosper. We need to be in the right position to receive, and we get into that position by following the conditions, by staying "on track."

My son, if you accept my words and store up my commands within you, turning your ear to wisdom and applying your heart to understanding, and if you call out for insight and cry aloud for understanding, and if you look for it as for silver and search for it as for hidden treasure . . . ~PROVERBS 2:1–4

The first two conditions we discover here are "accept" and "store up." Accepting God's Word is more than just hearing it—it also involves applying what we have heard (James 1:23–24). Not only that, but we are urged to store up God's commands within us, to gather them into the vault of our memory, as it were.

It would be pretty tough to remind you of the great weekend you had out on the West Coast—white water rapids, all the fresh salmon you could eat—if you were never there! We want to hear from God, but if we have not taken the time to store up his Word in our heart, what is there for the Holy Spirit to remind us of? (See John 14:26.)

Psalm 119:11 records David's commitment to God's conditions: "*I have hidden your word in my heart that I might not sin against you.*" Storing up and memorizing the

Word will keep your thought life on track as well as give the Holy Spirit the raw materials needed to guide you.

Turning your ear to wisdom and applying your heart to understanding . . . call out for insight and cry aloud for understanding. ~PROVERBS 2:2–4

When we want something that we think will benefit us we push pretty hard to go after it. If there is a concert or a game that we want to see but we do not know the dates or times or where to get tickets, we do whatever it takes to get that information. We scan the internet, make phone calls, drive across town.

How does your chasing after other "things" compare with how you go after God's Word? Do you call out for insight? What about cry aloud for understanding? Do you, as verse 4 adds, ". . . *look for it as for silver and search for it as for hidden treasure*"?

Really, this is a show stopper for me. Compare this to how our desires for "things" drive us to, say, go without food if we have to in order to save up money for what we want to do. When we get our sights set on a vacation or weekend trip, we pull up and out and call in as many resources as possible. What would our lives be like if our approach to God's Word was to go after it like buried treasure?

Then you will understand the fear of the Lord and find the knowledge of God. For the Lord gives wisdom, and from his mouth come knowledge and understanding. He holds victory in store for the upright, he is a shield to those whose walk is blameless, for he guards the course of the just and protects the way of his faithful ones. Then you will understand what is right and just and fair—every good path. For wisdom will enter your heart, and knowledge will be pleasant to your soul. Discretion will protect you, and understanding will guard you. ~PROVERBS 2:5–11

When we meet the conditions of God's Word, we position ourselves under his mighty hand of protection. We will be guided around all the traps and pitfalls the enemy tries to lure us into (Isaiah 54:17, 55:9; 2 Samuel 22:3; Psalm18:2, 144:2, 84:9 . . . the list goes on and on). God even gives his angels charge over us:

> *For He will give His angels [especial] charge over you to accompany and defend and preserve you in all your ways [of obedience and service].* ~PSALM 91:11 AMP

God wants to protect, guide, bless and prosper you. If you feel you're not experiencing this or you're receiving it only in small portions, do not allow the enemy to tell you that God is punishing you or that you're too bad to receive from God. Position yourself by following the conditions, and the blessing, power and peace of God will permeate every part of your being.

Keep your eyes on Jesus!

If . . . Then

*I am the Vine; you are the branches. Whoever lives in
Me and I in him bears much (abundant) fruit. However,
apart from Me [cut off from vital union with Me] you can
do nothing.* ~JOHN 15:5 AMP

Perhaps Jesus and his disciples were walking through
the countryside as they talked on that day. It wouldn't
have been uncommon for them to see vineyards as
they travelled, so Jesus' remarks would have made a quick
connection between what they saw around them and the
picture of spiritual life he was trying to help them see.

When a branch is broken off from its vine, it can't keep
on living. Oh, sure, maybe for a while it will stay green and
look like it's doing fine, but the fact that it's no longer
connected to its "life source" ensures that the appearance
of life will be a quickly fading reality.

What Jesus is saying here, if you haven't caught it yet,
is that if we are not "in him" and he is not "in us," we are
dead. Part of our life in Christ includes bearing fruit. Of
course, we don't really put out pineapples or pears; the
fruit we are to produce is in our character.

*But the fruit of the [Holy] Spirit [the work which His
presence within accomplishes] is love, joy (gladness),
peace, patience (an even temper, forbearance),*

> *kindness, goodness (benevolence), faithfulness,*
> *gentleness (meekness, humility), self-control (self-*
> *restraint, continence). Against such things there is no*
> *law [that can bring a charge].* ~GALATIANS 5:22–23 AMP

Are you struggling to live out your faith in Jesus, or have you decided to take a lukewarm attitude and live at a level that is lower than where you once were?

Bearing fruit takes energy, and an apple can't grow apart from its branch. When wind storms come through an orchard, the apples that aren't fully attached get knocked to the ground and their growing cycle is ended. We may be tempted to think that producing fruit in the spirit is just like that—once we're knocked down it's over. However, the difference is that, unlike an apple, we can re-attach our lives to Jesus, the Vine that provides our life source.

> *Do not be deceived and deluded and misled; God will*
> *not allow Himself to be sneered at (scorned, disdained,*
> *or mocked by mere pretensions or professions, or by His*
> *precepts being set aside.) [He inevitably deludes himself*
> *who attempts to delude God.] For whatever a man sows,*
> *that and that only is what he will reap.* ~GALATIANS 6:7 AMP

Vines do a good job of growing together. An untended patch could very well contain other plants that have sprouted up in the vicinity only to be gathered in by the vine's tendrils as they grow. Similarly, a branch that has become disconnected could easily be supported by the accumulated branches growing together around it, appearing as if it were no different than the rest. Ultimately, however, the absence of grapes will point to the fact that the branch is not part of the grapevine. And for as good as it may look, the lack of fruit being produced in one's life points to what has been seeded there as well.

Either make the tree sound (healthy and good), and its fruit sound (healthy and good), or make the tree rotten (diseased and bad), and its fruit rotten (diseased and bad); for the tree is known and recognized and judged by its fruit. ~MATTHEW 12:33 AMP

Being a "disciple" or follower of Jesus means that you are obedient to his Word. That obedience is how you stay "in him," attached to the vine and bearing appropriate fruit.

Jesus said, "If you hold to my teaching, you are really my disciples. Then you will know the truth, and the truth will set you free. ~JOHN 8:31-32

The two words I want you to consider today are "IF" and "THEN." IF you hold to the teaching of Jesus, THEN you will know the truth.

Do you feel like you're dying spiritually? Is there a connection that has been lost? Check your level of obedience. God will not give you the next set of directions if you haven't taken action on the ones already given.

This isn't a beating—I say this in love! If you feel beat up and wounded, run to the throne of God, not away from it, for that is where our lives are restored.

Let us then fearlessly and confidently and boldly draw near to the throne of grace (the throne of God's unmerited favor to us sinners), that we may receive mercy [for our failures] and find grace to help in good time for every need [appropriate help and well-timed help, coming just when we need it]. ~HEBREWS 4:16 AMP

God's Massive Love for You!

For God so greatly loved and dearly prized the world that He [even] gave up His only begotten (unique) Son, so that whoever believes in (trusts in, clings to, relies on) Him shall not perish (come to destruction, be lost) but have eternal (everlasting) life. ~JOHN 3:16 AMP

How do we show people we love them? What sorts of things do we do for those we love? I think it is a pretty universal fact that we like to spend time with our loved ones. We take pleasure in doing things like walking and dining together or just hanging out and talking.

Not only that, but we're protective of those we love. If someone were to try to rip them off in a deal or physically harm them, we'd step up to the plate and put a stop to it. We wouldn't just sit back! That would be nuts—we love this person; there is no way we would sit back and allow them to get hurt!! When we love somebody, we protect them.

When I take my nephews or niece to the park to play, we always end up having a great time laughing and building roads in the sand and swinging (until I get sick). We do a lot of laughing together. However, that laughter would quit pretty fast if anyone came to the park and attempted to hurt one of those precious children.

Really, if anyone would make a move to harm or even to touch one of those in my care, they would encounter some pretty wild results. A mother bear will attack anything that poses even a mild threat of danger to her cubs and that's the way I feel about my nephews and niece. At the first scent of trouble (or threat thereof) I'll move into defend and protect mode.

Are these my children? No. So if I act this way to protect them and I'm only their uncle, how much more do you think their mom or dad would react? Regardless of if we're followers of Jesus or not, we protect the ones we love.

If you then, evil as you are, know how to give good and advantageous gifts to your children, how much more will your Father Who is in heaven [perfect as He is] give good and advantageous things to those who keep on asking Him! ~MATTHEW 7:11 AMP

How colossal and ungraspable is God's love for his creation! God's love for each one of us is far bigger than our love for anyone or anything. If we look after those who we love, how much more does God care for and look after those he loves? Over and over again in the Bible, God tells us not to panic, or get chased into doubt. He loves us, immensely! When we were still living out our sinful ways, Jesus died for us (Romans 5:6). God loves us so much that he not only told us about that love in his Word but he also acted on it by giving Jesus to take our punishment (1 Peter 2:24).

For Christ [the Messiah Himself] died for sins once for all, the Righteous for the unrighteous (the Just for the unjust, the Innocent for the guilty), that He might bring us to God. In His human body He was put to death, but He was made alive in the spirit . . . ~1 PETER 3:18 AMP

Trust him—that's your part of the deal.

God's love for you is so massive, he has put reminders throughout the Bible that he'll take care of you. For instance, check out these passages: Isaiah 41:9–13 and Psalms 91, 121, and 23. Really, the list could go on and on, but start with these, and as you read them, think about how MASSIVE God's love is for you!

Front and Centre

We reserve our best attention for those things we deem priorities in our lives. If we randomly asked a person on the street to name some of their priorities, we would probably expect to hear answers such as family, friends, job, health; however, to simply label something as a priority really means very little until the facts are proven by actions.

God's Word should not take a back seat to other things on the list of what we feel is important. We have to keep God's Word front and centre. Just like many other areas of our lives, if it's not in the schedule, it just won't get done!

I meditate on your precepts and consider your ways. I delight in your decrees; I will not neglect your word.
~PSALM 119:15–16

Here are some practical steps to help you keep God's Word front and centre in your life:

1. THINK ABOUT IT. *"I meditate on your precepts."*

It seems as life gets faster and more and more great books are put out on the market, time to read is tight. Time to actually think about what is being said and applied to one's own life is even rarer.

When reading the Word, take some time to stop and daydream about it. We daydream about many things, so why not on God's Word as well? How does this passage apply to me? How can I use this today? Let your imagination go—that's what it means to "meditate" on God's Word. *Think* about it.

2. ACCEPT THE WORD. *"I . . . consider your ways."*

Take into consideration what the Word is saying. When we just read over a passage like we'd read a cheap novel, really what we're doing (besides robbing ourselves of taking into consideration what it means to us and for us) is showing disrespect. If you don't see what's important to God but rather treat it as "just another thing to read," you're not accepting or respecting his Word.

3. CELEBRATE GOD'S WORD. *"I delight in your decrees."*

Do you ever celebrate the Word? It's a good time! When you know God's Word is true about you (and for you) and that it applies to every part of your life, celebrating is just a natural step to take.

Every time you have a prayer answered, every time something goes right, remind yourself that you are qualified by the finished work of Jesus. The more you magnify Jesus as your righteousness, the more you connect to wholeness and leave lack and all its destructive power behind. The more you remind

yourself that Jesus is enough, the more He becomes
your everything.[1]

4. REMEMBER. *"I will not neglect your word."*

Don't forget what you have read. Be creative. Bring
back to your mind the joy, the peace you had when you
read the Word. Write out part of a verse or a few verses on
a small card that you can carry with you or store them in
your phone or other handheld device. Then when you have
a spare moment waiting at a red light, in an elevator or at
lunch hour, review what you read in your study time. Keep
bringing that Word to mind throughout the day.

Anyone who listens to the word but does not do what it
says is like a man who looks at his face in a mirror and,
after looking at himself, goes away and immediately
forgets what he looks like. ~JAMES 1:23–24

Remembering means putting the instructions into
action. If you read a certain passage but then neglect to do
what it says, do you really remember it? Remembering is
doing. (Don't forget!) Stay full of the Word!

I have hidden your word in my heart that I might not sin
against you. ~PSALM 119:11

Whatever your plans are, keep God's Word front and
centre. You'll be amazed at how much simpler life gets
when you find you don't have to do everything yourself!

Grace, peace and joy be yours in massive amounts as
you go into this day.

---

[1] James B. Richards, *Breaking the Cycle* (Denver: Legacy Publishers,
2003), p. 108

Not Disqualified

There is a really good chance that before you reached the noon hour today you messed up in some area of your thoughts, actions or words. It's great to think about being perfect, but it isn't likely we will achieve it. At the same time, however, there is no excuse for not trying to attain or at least aim for it.

When we make a mistake, the weight of our error can silence us, effectively shutting our mouths to the confession of God's Word. The words of the enemy ring in our ears: "Loser, you blew it this time. There is no turning back—you are a hypocrite!"

But the moment we begin to feel worthless is the very time to remember and understand who we are in Christ and who he is in us. It's in those times that we have to speak God's Word boldly, knowing it hasn't changed. We may have changed, our situation may have changed, but the Word of God hasn't.

". . . but the word of the Lord stands forever." And this is the word that was preached to you. ~1 PETER 1:25

Every good and perfect gift is from above, coming down from the Father of the heavenly lights, who does not change like shifting shadows. ~JAMES 1:17

As we process our feelings of remorse, we need to speak God's Word out loud and clear, confessing the promises of God.

Let us then approach the throne of grace with confidence, so that we may receive mercy and find grace to help us in our time of need. ~HEBREWS 4:16

If we confess our sins, he is faithful and just and will forgive us our sins and purify us from all unrighteousness. ~1 JOHN 1:9

In Christ Jesus we are forgiven. Jesus died a sinner's death in our place. When Jesus hung on the cross, he shouted out, "My God, why have you forsaken me?" He wasn't just quoting a verse; he was experiencing separation and rejection from God because he literally became the sins of the world. In this way, Jesus completed the requirements to pay the price for our shortfalls (Romans 8:1–4, 2 Corinthians 5:21, Hebrews 9:12, 1 Peter 2:24) and now our debt is paid in full. It's a "done deal," for the covenant has been made and can't be broken. In Christ Jesus we never have to be slaves to sin again! (Romans 6:6, 16–18, 22).

It is encouraging to note that the New Covenant wasn't made with you or me—God made the covenant with Jesus. If the covenant was between God and me, I could break the covenant or fail to keep my part and thereby lose all the benefits. The thing that makes the covenant sure is that it was made with Jesus. He completed the requirements (Romans 8:1–4). Since he died and was raised up in righteousness it cannot be altered or changed. In fact, Jesus has taken every step ahead of us, paving the road that we should walk and showing us the power that works in us. He is the perfect model.

We are now righteous in God's sight, but that doesn't stop the enemy from attempting to block us from walking in the freedom that Jesus has given us. So if you've made a major mistake and feel like you should never share the Word of God with anybody again, stop it! Those feelings are from the enemy; he wants to discourage you and push you back into the past. When you start to question—"Who am I to share the Word with somebody after what I did?— remind yourself (and the enemy) that you are not down for the count! To be forgiven means getting a fresh start to try again.

Look at the Apostle Peter. He was a big talker, but when it came down to proving it with actions, he had nothing left to say (Matthew 26:35, 70).

Then Peter remembered the word Jesus had spoken: "Before the rooster crows, you will disown me three times." And he went outside and wept bitterly. ~MATTHEW 26:75

This was no trivial misdemeanour, and Peter obviously felt the weight of his failure. Yet he experienced firsthand the power of forgiveness and grace available to all of us as he gets reinstated by Jesus (John 21:7) and by the power of the Holy Spirit begins again to speak out.

Then Peter stood up with the Eleven, raised his voice and addressed the crowd . . . ~ACTS 2:14–36

Peter failed royally, but he didn't allow that mistake to keep him from being all that God had planned for him.

If you think you have stumbled too many times to ever be used by God again, then you do not understand what Jesus did for you on the cross. You are a new creation; the old is gone, the past has no hold on you! (2 Corinthians 5:17; Galatians 2:20). As a born again believer, you have been forgiven.

> *Now if we died with Christ, we believe that we will also live with him. For we know that since Christ was raised from the dead, he cannot die again; death no longer has mastery over him. The death he died, he died to sin once for all; but the life he lives, he lives to God. In the same way, count yourselves dead to sin but alive to God in Christ Jesus.* ~ROMANS 6:8–11

> *For Christ died for sins once for all, the righteous for the unrighteous, to bring you to God. He was put to death in the body but made alive by the Spirit. . .* ~1 PETER 3:18

You are qualified in Christ Jesus! Do not allow the enemy to use anybody or anything to throw you off course. When you asked Jesus into your life, you stepped into the covenant; you became a part of it. Nothing can separate you from God's love (Romans 8:37–39), so you can go into this day with joy and boldness, forgetting what lies behind (Philippians 3:13) and walking out your new life (Romans 6:4).

The enemy will try to use anybody and anything to disqualify you, but the truth is he can't disqualify you. It's all a cheap trick. The devil is a liar (John 8:44). There isn't a single bit of truth in him—not even the slightest hint of truth! When he says anything, it's a lie!

So now it's time to get up and get going.

God doesn't see you as a failure; why would you want to see yourself that way? Keep your eyes on Jesus, speak

God's Word continually and stand on those promises
(Philippians 4:8; Hebrews 12:1–3).

*No, in all these things we are more than conquerors
through him who loved us.* ~Romans 8:37

*To them God has chosen to make known among the
Gentiles the glorious riches of this mystery, which is
Christ in you, the hope of glory.* ~Colossians 1:27

You are not disqualified—not a chance! Have a
powerful day, Saint!

Real Time 4-Wheel Drive?

While I was waiting for a red light to turn green, a vehicle pulled up in the lane beside me and moved a little ahead of where I was. As I glanced at the vehicle I saw on the back panel chrome letters that read "Real Time 4WD."

"Real time?" I mused out loud. It's like when someone uses the phrase "at this point in time"—at which other point in time would you be? Then it struck me. When we dwell too long on the past or are fixated on the future, we actually *are* living (or are at least making a sorry attempt to live) in another point in time. And either one of those is equally futile.

Jesus referred to himself as the "I AM." Not the "I Was" or the "I'm Going to Be"—the "I AM." His power, peace, provision and protection are given to us in the current moment, not in the failures of yesterday or the projections of what might be or could be. We need to live this day to the full in God's grace. As we do, then we are prepared and shaped for what the next day will bring.

Psalm 91 shows us how to live in the now. Let's begin with verse 1:

*He who dwells in the shelter of the Most High will rest in
the shadow of the Almighty.*

Resting in the Lord is focusing on him. Resting means
knowing that all his promises to us are affirmed with a
"Yes!" (2 Corinthians 1:20). Alternatively, when we are not
at rest, choosing rather to worry about life, we are
inadvertently clarifying what and wherein we are placing
our trust and where we are not (Proverbs 3:5–6, Jeremiah
29:11).

Having a vision for where you feel your life could be
going is a good thing. However, that vision can be the very
thing that stops you from living today in a restful, trusting
way.

Sometimes our plans and dreams can cause us to try to
live ahead of where we are at, taking us out of real time.
This can cause blindness and deafness to the Spirit and
disregard for the simple steps that must be taken before
one is prepared for what that vision requires.

Verse 2 provides us with a tool for re-focusing. Our
mouths need to be used to speak the truth, the direction we
need to go according to God's Word.

*I will say of the Lord, "He is my refuge and my fortress,
my God, in whom I trust."*

Verses 3 to 6 shows us how we are to boldly confess our
protection and confidence in God.

*Surely he will save you from the fowler's snare and from
the deadly pestilence. He will cover you with his
feathers, and under his wings you will find refuge; his
faithfulness will be your shield and rampart. You will not
fear the terror of night, nor the arrow that flies by day,*

nor the pestilence that stalks in the darkness, nor the plague that destroys at midday.

Verses 7 and 8:

A thousand may fall at your side, ten thousand at your right hand, but it will not come near you. You will only observe with your eyes and see the punishment of the wicked.

How much perseverance would it take to endure while a thousand or ten thousand fall at your side? You need to have faith—not just in your head but faith that is firmly planted in your heart and that comes out of your mouth. Don't wait until things start falling apart around you; speaking your faith needs to start today.

Every promise we have read in the first 8 verses is conditional. They won't be fulfilled because you have merely read about them or heard about them; you need to meet the condition:

If you make the Most High your dwelling—even the Lord, who is my refuge . . . ~v. 9

The ultimate shelter we can find is to live in God's love.
The Psalm goes on to tell us,

...then no harm will befall you, no disaster will come near your tent. ~v. 10

Living in real time involves blooming where you are planted. Real time is now. Forget about the mistakes of yesterday; quit trying to correct something that you can't change. Change the things you can and live this day to the full, just the way Jesus intended you to: in his protection, peace, provision and power.

You will keep in perfect peace him whose mind is steadfast, because he trusts in you. ~ISAIAH 26:3

Personalize Psalm 91 and speak it daily. Staying in God and in his Word is how we "drive" in "Real Time."

Sitt'n and Soak'n or Digg'n and Doin'?

We are living in a time when we can access the Word of God just about any place we go. Bookstores carry Bibles, the internet is loaded with great sites to not only read God's Word but hear it read to us. Really, so many people who call themselves "Christian" hear a lot of the Word, but how much are they digging into it?

That's the easy question. But what about the harder question—what are YOU doing with God's Word?

Are you doing what you have been taught? Do you even know what it says after hearing it over and over again? Are you just sitting around and soaking up as much teaching as you can, going to as many functions as you can just to say you've been there, or are you digging deep into God's Word and looking for areas to be obedient to it?

Why do you call Me, Lord, Lord, and do not [practice] what I tell you? For everyone who comes to Me and listens to My words [in order to heed their teaching] and does them, I will show you what he is like: He is like a man building a house, who dug and went down deep and laid a foundation upon the rock; and when a flood arose, the torrent broke against that house and could not shake

*or move it, because it had been securely built or founded
on a rock. But he who merely hears and does not practice
doing My words is like a man who built a house on the
ground without a foundation, against which the torrent
burst, and immediately it collapsed and fell, and the
breaking and ruin of that house was great. ~LUKE 6:46–49 AMP*

Digging deep is more than a quick skim through a
devotional book and more than reading the first chapter of
Genesis (or Psalms or Matthew or John) over again for the
fifteenth day in a row. Ever seen a hungry dog going after a
steak?

Getting into God's Word, like learning from any book
or teacher, involves focused time and effort, not only to
study and pray and actually think through understanding
it, but also then to apply it, use it and walk out what it says.
That is how we get rock solid faith, so that when tough
times come—and they will—we will not need to worry
because we are already rooted in truth (Ephesians 3:17;
Colossians 2:7; James 1:21; 1 Peter 5:9; 1 John 2:27).

Anyone who wants to build a good house is going to
make sure that the ground underneath it is stable. They'll
dig deep into the bedrock, and if need be, they will pound
pilings way down until they reach solid ground. There is no
other way for the foundation of the house to be secure.
When the strong winds and storms blow, the residents of
the house will have no concern because they know what it
is built on and what it is rooted in.

The same is true for our lives. It is easy to say we love
God and trust him when the lights are on, but how strong
is that confession when the lights are snuffed out? Even
when it feels like the bottom has dropped out, is it possible
to praise God in the middle of the darkness?

I have hidden your word in my heart that I might not sin against you. ~PSALM 119:11

YES! it is completely possible if your foundation (belief system) is well-established in your heart, your mouth and your mind. When the storms of life blow, you will stand firm because of that solid foundation. And that foundation is built by daily hiding God's Word in your heart—not just sitt'n and soak'n, but digg'n and doin'!

1. How do you dig deep and build a good base?

Develop a habit of spending time in the Bible every day. Set a time. I find first thing in the morning is the best time for me, as it allows me to focus and set my priorities on Jesus. I start the day confessing who I am as his child and who he is as my God.

Memorizing Scripture is another great way to energize and encourage yourself. Throughout the day, when trails and tests come, you can speak God's Word and his peace will fill the situation you are facing. God's Word leads us in his ways rather than our own.

Share your insights with someone. Seek out and develop a friendship with an older Christian (who is a proven man or woman of God) so that you can have someone in your life to bounce your thoughts off of and be accountable to for applying and using what you already know, regardless of how little you think that may be.

2. How do you "Hear" and then "Do"?

Nike came out years ago with their slogan "Just Do It." I can't tell you how often that rings in my thoughts. The Holy Spirit speaks to each one of us every day. I think we miss so many blessings and opportunities to be a blessing because we don't listen or we write off what we have heard with a "No, that can't be." Too often, we end up walking out of a God-ordained meeting with someone that we could have spoken words of life to. We have to be obedient to the Word of God.

When you are reading God's Word or thinking about it (meditating on it) and something seems especially clear to you, then keep that thought going and do as you are being lead (told) to do. Being obedient to what we know we should do is the essence of hearing and doing, and it is also part of building the foundation that prevents us from getting knocked down and out in the middle of the storms of life.

> *But be doers of the Word [obey the message], and not merely listeners to it, betraying yourselves [into deception by reasoning contrary to the Truth]. For if anyone only listens to the Word without obeying it and being a doer of it, he is like a man who looks carefully at his [own] natural face in a mirror; For he thoughtfully observes himself, and then goes off and promptly forgets what he was like. ~JAMES 1:22–24 AMP*

That's a little bizarre. Who forgets what they look like?

Sadly, we can probably all say it's true of us. It's very possible to hear good teaching or have a powerful time in the Word but not allow it to affect our actions towards others. We get up and walk away, not remembering what we were just shown.

3. How do we look in a mirror and not forget what we look like?

> *But he who looks carefully into the faultless law, the [law] of liberty, and is faithful to it and perseveres in looking*

into it, being not a heedless listener who forgets but an active doer [who obeys], he shall be blessed in his doing (his life of obedience). If anyone thinks himself to be religious (piously observant of the external duties of his faith) and does not bridle his tongue but deludes his own heart, this person's religious service is worthless (futile, barren). External religious worship [religion as it is expressed in outward acts] that is pure and unblemished in the sight of God the Father is this: to visit and help and care for the orphans and widows in their affliction and need, and to keep oneself unspotted and uncontaminated from the world. ~JAMES 1:25–27 AMP

God's Word is powerful and active.

For the Word that God speaks is alive and full of power [making it active, operative, energizing, and effective]; it is sharper than any two-edged sword, penetrating to the dividing line of the breath of life (soul) and [the immortal] spirit, and of joints and marrow [of the deepest parts of our nature], exposing and sifting and analyzing and judging the very thoughts and purposes of the heart. ~HEBREWS 4:12 AMP

As we read, study and memorize the Word, we are becoming more and more like Jesus. That's what God wants. He wants us to be like Jesus, for we were created in his image (Genesis 1:26) and we have been given the mind of Christ (1 Corinthians 2:16).

The mirror of God's Word reflects our *true identity*, but when we walk away from it and start acting like the "old self" and allowing others to make us feel like the "old us," we are forgetting what we just saw! Scripture opens our eyes us to see WHO we are and WHOSE we are, not who we used to be or who others would like to say we are.

- *You are a child of the Most High God. (John 1:12–13)*

- *You have been chosen by God. (Isaiah 41:9)*

- *You been bought with the blood of Jesus. (1 Corinthians 6:20, 1 Peter 2:24)*

- *You are anointed. (2 Corinthians 1:21–22)*

- *You are blessed with EVERY spiritual blessing. (Ephesians 1:3)*

Never allow anyone to tell you anything else!
Sitt'n and soak'n is OK, but dig in, and get doing.

> *Thank you, Jesus, for your grace and mercy to me. Thank you, Lord, for your love. Thank you for the Holy Spirit who leads me into all truth (John 14:26), who guarantees you are coming back for me (2 Corinthians 1:22) and who gives life to my body (Romans 8:11). You are my God, and today I choose to serve you with all my heart, I choose to speak your Word, I choose to act in love to those I encounter. You alone, Father, are worthy of all praise, glory and honor. In Jesus' name, Amen.*

Watch the Gauge

It would be great to sail through life problem free, but we well know the realities that accompany that hope. We have a limited, fleshy body and we live in a sinful world where the choices of others, as well as our own, affect our environment and the circumstances we live within.

Dark nights, overwhelming situations and the accompanying feelings of despair have not been reserved for just a select few. Because we have an enemy who is out to steal, kill and destroy (John 10:10), we are all going to face times of trail, seasons when life just simply seems to be at a stand-still.

Understand this: God said, "Never will I leave you; never will I forsake you" (Hebrews 13:5). The enemy would like you to believe that you are alone and too far gone for God to even pay any attention to you. However, that is not the case.

He who did not spare his own Son, but gave him up for us all—how will he not also, along with him, graciously give us all things? ~ROMANS 8:32

Jesus said,

I have told you these things, so that in me you may have peace. In this world you will have trouble. But take heart! I have overcome the world. ~JOHN 16:33

"Fret not." "Fear not." "Do not worry." Don't get into those useless traps! Jesus wasn't making suggestions—these are commands.

What can you do when it feels like you are out on your own in a hopeless situation? First, you need to stop allowing feelings to tell you how to respond and allow God's Word to accurately show you the truth of that situation.

Pilots are trained to fly by the gauges, not by what they feel. If there is ever a question between which one to believe—their emotions or the gauges—they are trained to always go with the gauges. In the same way, when you get caught between your emotions and God's Word, always go with God's Word regardless of how you feel or think or what others are saying around you. Side with God's Word; keep your eyes on the gauges.

Gauges in planes have been known to fail. That's where the similarities end. God's Word is never wrong—never has been, never will be. So what is a person to do in tough times when emotions are raw and direction seems scattered? Proverbs 3:5–6 shows us the steps we need to take when life seems to be going in a downward spiral:

Trust in the Lord with all your heart and lean not on your own understanding; in all your ways acknowledge him, and he will make your paths straight.

We are supposed to trust the Lord. God knows you. He knows what you need (Psalm 139:1–4), He has an awesome plan for your life (Jeremiah 29:11) and he wants you to succeed and not fail. We are his ambassadors on this planet (2 Corinthians 5:20). God has made us righteous in Jesus (2 Corinthians 5:21) and he has given us the Holy Spirit in our hearts as a guarantee of what is to come (2 Corinthians 1:22). God can be fully trusted.

When life seems to be a burden and your feelings are telling you to "give up and give in," look to the gauge; look to God and not to the feelings that are screaming for attention. Trust in the Lord with all your heart.

In times of stress and struggles a half-hearted attempt at the Word will do you more damage then good. If you approach God's promises thinking that some are true and the others are debatable, the enemy will capitalize on that doubt and bring it to full bloom. If you don't trust God's Word, you don't trust him at all (James 1:6–8).

The second step is to "*lean not on your own understanding.*"

Trusting God means placing confidence not in what you see but in what you do not see (2 Corinthians 4:18). Just like I mentioned before, when a pilot has to make a choice between the gauges or his or her feelings, the gauges are always to win out. Do not lean on the way you think things are going; stick with God's Word for accurate readings.

Thirdly, verse 6 goes on to instruct: "*in all your ways acknowledge him.*"

Acknowledging the Lord is how we keep his Word front and centre. As you go about your day, talk to God and thank him for his provision, for your health, your job, just simply for giving you another day to give him thanks.

Be joyful always; pray continually; give thanks in all circumstances, for this is God's will for you in Christ Jesus. Do not put out the Spirit's fire. ~1 THESSALONIANS 5:16–19

Lastly, when you are trusting fully and not making judgment calls based on the way you think or see, as you keep God and his Word front and center, he promises that then "he will make your paths straight." You will begin to see situations differently. You will act and not "re-act."

God's Word is life and health to all who find it (Proverbs 4:22).

(For further encouragement, take some time to read Isaiah 41:9–13.)

We Are More
Romans 8:28–39

If I were to go out for lunch with you and tell you that everything you have been led to believe is a lie, how would you handle it?

Everything your parents told you about your entrance into your family, about how they named you and raised you, was just an elaborate story put together to make you feel special. Your teachers were paid off to give you good marks. Your friends? Paid off as well. Yep, the whole thing was a hoax, and you have been taken for the ride of your life. How would you handle that? Would you just sit there and allow me to continue on with the lie?

Would you get up, point your finger in my face, and scream "Liar!"? Would you freak out in shock and say, "Well, I thought . . ." and then go on to tell me how you had believed your parents?

As unbelievable as the scenario sounds, that's pretty much what the devil tries to pull on every one us. He comes in with his lies (as far-fetched as they may be) and tries to tell us that we will never measure up, that we will never make it and that God is mad at us. However, when we know the truth about who we are as chosen, called, anointed and righteous children of God, the devil's lies are easily defeated. When we speak God's Word, stand on God's Word and know God's Word, we become more than conquerors.

WE KNOW:

And we know that in all things God works for the good of those who love him, who have been called according to his purpose. ~ROMANS 8:28

Do you know that God is for you and that in everything (if you allow him to) he works for the good of those who love him, those who have been called, with purpose and on purpose, and included in his plan?

I hope your answer is Yes. And that it is not "...yes," but "YES!"

This knowledge needs to be rooted deep in our hearts so that when the storms of life rage around us it keeps growing. Hosea 4:6a notes: "*My people are destroyed from lack of knowledge.*" When you spend time in the Word and with God in prayer, your knowledge is being strengthened. Time in the Word shows you who God is and who you are in him. The more we know about what God says about himself, about us and about the situations we face, the stronger we become and the less opportunity the enemy has to waylay us with his lies of destruction.

Isaiah 41:9–10 reminds us,

I took you from the ends of the earth, from its farthest corners I called you. I said, "You are my servant"; I have chosen you and have not rejected you. So do not fear, for I am with you; do not be dismayed, for I am your God. I will strengthen you and help you; I will uphold you with my righteous right hand. My frame was not hidden from you when I was made in the secret place. When I was woven together in the depths of the earth, your eyes saw my unformed body. All the days ordained for me were written in your book before one of them came to be. ~PSALM 139:15–16

Paul began Romans 8:28 with the phrase "And we know." When we know and understand our purpose— God's purpose for our purpose—then storms and tough times take on a different tone. That is not to say we eagerly anticipate or wish for those trials or that we are always having a great time in the middle of the storm. We are simply and confidently aware that God has a plan when we love him and trust him and continue to stay focused on his Word no matter what our physical eyes see.

Stop for a minute here and ask yourself, "Do I know, not just in my head but in my heart?"

GOD KNOWS:

For those God foreknew he also predestined to be conformed to the likeness of his Son, that he might be the firstborn among many brothers. And those he predestined, he also called; those he called, he also justified; those he justified, he also glorified. ~ROMANS 8:29–30

"Predestined" can also be thought of as "pre-designed." God has not only charted a map for our lives but also given us a guidance system that leads us perfectly on the paths he has planned for us. That system consists of his Word, the Holy Spirit and our direct line of communication: prayer. All three work together. When we follow God's plan for our lives, we show up at the right places at the right time and the right people come across our path at the perfect moment.

When tough times do come, we know that because God has a plan and we are following that plan he will provide the answer to that position. If we allow him to, he can turn anything—any weapon, any problem—into a tool that will bring us only higher, up to the next step as opposed to losing any ground (Isaiah 54:17).

THE QUESTION:

What, then, shall we say in response to this? If God is for us, who can be against us? ~ROMANS 8:31

Then Paul goes on to say, "*If God is for us...*" You really have to settle this question in your heart once and for all. "Is God for you?" If you do not know the answer to that question, then every time you feel the lights go out in your life and it seems the bottom has fallen out and you can't sense God's presence, the enemy will toss it in your face and dig at your doubts with "Is God really for you?" Read on . . .

He who did not spare his own Son, but gave him up for us all—how will he not also, along with him, graciously give us all things? ~ROMANS 8:32

This is the answer you need to know deep inside your being. God did not even spare his only Son. God charged him with our sin and shame so that we could go free and live in the power and authority of his name.

Is God for you? YES, YES, YES!

Who will bring any charge against those whom God has chosen? It is God who justifies. Who is he that condemns? Christ Jesus, who died—more than that, who was raised to life—is at the right hand of God and is also interceding for us. Who shall separate us from the love of Christ? Shall trouble or hardship or persecution or famine or nakedness or danger or sword? As it is written: "For your sake we face death all day long; we are considered as sheep to be slaughtered." ~ROMANS 8:33–36

THE ANSWER:

No, in all these things we are more than conquerors through him who loved us. For I am convinced that neither death nor life, neither angels nor demons, neither the present nor the future, nor any powers, 39neither height nor depth, nor anything else in all creation, will be able to separate us from the love of God that is in Christ Jesus our Lord. ~ROMANS 8:37–39

Convinced: positive, confident, knowing for sure.

Are you convinced that neither death nor life, neither angels nor demons, neither the present nor the future, nor any powers, neither height nor depth, nor anything else in all creation, will be able to separate us from the love of God that is in Christ Jesus our Lord? Have you ever noticed when you are feeling down how it seems like God has left you? That when things get really tough it seems like your prayers go as high as the ceiling then bounce back to the floor?

Don't be fooled! Be convinced that nothing can separate you from God's love. No matter what you are facing, no matter what your eyes see physically, you have been pre-designed with the ability to overcome all of the lies of the enemy.

Be convinced—YOU are more than a CONQUEROR in Christ!

Park It at 37

Many times when I read something that I have read before, the Holy Spirit brings out powerful insights that I apparently overlooked the other times. This morning, like many mornings, I stopped by Psalm 37 on my way to Proverbs. This Psalm has been of great help in the past, and this morning was no exception.

Pull over. Park it. Take some time with me as we walk through this Psalm. I want to show you what I saw today.

Often we complicate our lives by doing things that God never intended for us to do. We are guilty of getting caught up in stuff that is clearly been marked off limits for us. On the other side of that, the very actions we are supposed to take are the ones we don't. Mixed up, you say? Oh yes!

Psalm 37 will refresh those areas that we are not to mess with and renew the areas we are supposed to be taking action in. Here we go:

> *Do not fret because of evil men or be envious of those who do wrong; . . . ~v. 1*

Some days it looks like the people who cheat and lie and steal are getting ahead. Whatever they are doing and whatever they are into, however, is really none of your business. "Do not fret." In other words, don't "freak out" over stuff, don't panic, quit getting all worked up about it. Why?

. . . for like the grass they will soon wither, like green plants they will soon die away. ~v. 2

Sure, for now it looks like they are winning. But the clock is ticking. Becoming distressed over what we see will only set us up for failure.

Trust in the Lord and do good; dwell in the land and enjoy safe pasture. ~v. 3

Just do what you know you are supposed to be doing. Trust God's plan for your life; it's not as if he is unaware of what is going on around you.

1. Don't freak out.
2. Trust God and do good stuff.
3. Delight yourself in the Lord.

Delight yourself in the Lord and he will give you the desires of your heart. ~v. 4

Celebrate. Maintain a thankful heart. Many times we complain about work, health, relationships and the list goes on. Complaining is the exact opposite of what this verse is telling us to do. Thank God for your home, your apartment, your bed, your toothbrush and that you can keep your teeth in good condition. Again, the list is endless. Just be thankful about everything you have and for the great friends in your life. God wants to give you the pure desires of your heart; however, thankfulness is key.

A lot of what goes on in our daily lives is pretty much self-inflicted. Because we accept worry, stress is normal. We often trust our jobs and our paycheques more than we trust God. This combination opens the way to complaining, which puts a plug in the system and actually holds up the desires that our heart yearns for.

> *Commit your way to the Lord [roll and repose each care of your load on Him]; trust (lean on, rely on, and be confident) also in Him and He will bring it to pass.*
> *~PSALM 37:5 AMP*

Verse 6 explains what happens when we commit our way to the Lord,

> *He will make your righteousness shine like the dawn, the justice of your cause like the noonday sun.*

Also,

> *The path of the righteous is like the first gleam of dawn, shining ever brighter till the full light of day.* *~PROVERBS 4:18*

Are you tired of stumbling around, wondering what is next or how it is going to happen? Commit your way to the Lord.

Verse: 7 tells us the next step:

> *Be still before the Lord and wait patiently for him; do not fret when men succeed in their ways, when they carry out their wicked schemes.* *~PSALM 37:7*

Patience is a tough attribute to hold on to when your job or your bank or the TV—the whole world, it seems—is shouting, "Faster! Faster!" It is equally tough to maintain when people call you down or make up scenarios that never happened so they can get ahead, or at very least, set you back. To "wait patiently" often feels like the wrong answer when your human instinct is screaming at you to step up, get the record straight and stand in your defence.

But go back and read verse 7 again. God has a plan for your life. He knows what is going on. It is not like something slips by him and he is as surprised as you are when something goes down. His faithfulness is a solid place for our trust and patience to rest.

Then verse 8 clarifies the actions we do need to take:

Refrain from anger and turn from wrath; do not fret—it leads only to evil.

We are to refrain from anger. God's Word tells us to love our enemies in spite of what they are saying and doing. We need to walk away from the instinct to strike back.

You have heard that it was said, "Love your neighbor and hate your enemy." But I tell you: Love your enemies and pray for those who persecute you. ~MATTHEW 5:43–44

Anger, striking back or wanting to unleash our wrath only brings us to the level of the attacker, and maybe even lower—it drags us into sin. We are not to judge. Actually, we make horrible judges, especially in cases that involve us personally. Take a look at how Luke put it:

Do not judge, and you will not be judged. Do not condemn, and you will not be condemned. Forgive, and you will be forgiven. ~LUKE 6:37

Psalm 37:9 says,

For evil men will be cut off, but those who hope in the Lord will inherit the land.

Is life getting a little too hectic for you? Are you feeling overwhelmed and underpowered? Park it at 37! Take these six simple steps and read the passage over again (many times), asking the Holy Spirit for help in understanding how to apply them specifically to your life today.

1. Don't fret.
2. Trust God and continue doing good, no matter what.
3. Delight yourself in the Lord; be a thankful person.
4. Commit your way to the Lord; trust him completely.
5. Be still, patient before the Lord.
6. Do not allow anger to get the better of you.

Choices

Every day we are faced with choices that determine whether we move ahead or slide backwards. If we want to grow up in our walk with Jesus, we must learn how to make right choices and then follow through, no matter what discomfort it may bring.

> *In fact, though by this time you ought to be teachers, you need someone to teach you the elementary truths of God's Word all over again. You need milk, not solid food! Anyone who lives on milk, being still an infant, is not acquainted with the teaching about righteousness. But solid food is for the mature, who by constant use have trained themselves to distinguish good from evil.*
> *~HEBREWS 5:12–14*

Peter wrote,

> *Like newborn babies you should crave (thirst for, earnestly desire) the pure (unadulterated) spiritual milk, that by it you may be nurtured and grow unto [completed] salvation.* *~1 PETER 2:2 AMP*

Choices get easier, not just with age, but with maturity in God's Word. Making right choices every moment of the day becomes more and more possible as we develop in our walk with the Lord, and wise decisions are generated by planting God's Word in our hearts and letting it come out of our mouths.

Here is how to get started in that direction:

1. Ask God to give you insight into his will for your life.

Ask for help to clarify your thoughts and emotions so you can distinguish between choosing what is best from what is merely good. That's asking for wisdom.

2. Share what you have learned.

One good test of how well you know something is to try to teach it to someone else—not just to dump information but to actually make a clear presentation. Reading good books and listening to great teachers is fantastic, but it gets even better when we can turn around and multiply those teachings by instructing someone else.

3. Don't just skim the top and grab the easy-to-swallow points in your study of God's Word.

Dive in, go deep and look for ways that the Word can be immediately applied to your life.

Leaders are readers and listeners. Podcasts are in abundance and the internet makes it possible to connect with great teachers from around the world. It's not just about gathering information, it's what you do with that intake that makes the time spent worthwhile.

4. Don't be your own worst bully.

I care very little if I am judged by you or by any human court; indeed, I do not even judge myself. . . . It is the Lord who judges me. ~1 CORINTHIANS 4:3–4

We naturally look for a place to lay the blame when things don't work out, but the truth is we are prone to being too hard on ourselves as well as other people. Negative self-talk is destructive, for it will lead you down paths you were never meant to go. God knows our hearts and our motives. He alone knows the entire truth, so let him do the evaluation with his Word.

We live by faith, not by sight. ~2 CORINTHIANS 5:7

Ask the Lord to help you be led more by the Spirit than by the flesh. Trust God to help you, knowing that he will bring things to pass no matter how unlikely they currently look.

5. Step up to the plate.

In the same way, let your light shine before men, that they may see your good deeds and praise your Father in heaven. ~MATTHEW 5:16

Don't wait for someone to call you with an opportunity to serve—take the initiative and volunteer to bring blessings to others. Where does your church, community club or friendship group need help? If you don't know, make it your business to know. If you are aware of a need, then get to it. Jesus gave us an example by washing the feet of the disciples (John 13:14); if you want to be great for God, learn how to be a great servant to those around you (Mark 9:35).

We have all been given gifts to use to build up those around us. Even the skills and abilities we take for granted or dismiss as not as good or special as someone else's gifts are valuable tools in God's hands.

As iron sharpens iron, so one man sharpens another.
~PROVERBS 27:17

For instance, you may well know more about the Word of God than the person you work next to.

Study and be eager and do your utmost to present yourself to God approved (tested by trial), a workman who has no cause to be ashamed, correctly analyzing and accurately dividing [rightly handling and skillfully teaching] the Word of Truth. *~2 TIMOTHY 2:15 AMP*

Use what's in your hand right now! Don't wait for the "if only" clause to kick in—take what you have and sow it. You can encourage someone at work, a cashier or the person pumping the gas into your car. Every one of us has the ability to speak a kind word; if that's all you feel you have to give, then give it!

I can do everything through him who gives me strength.
~PHILIPPIANS 4:13

Don't stand in one spot waiting for all the right conditions to fall into place—that's probably not going to happen. Go with what you've got where you're at. It's not the size of the tasks you accomplish, it's the heart behind the act that scores the reward.

The ball is in your court and you need to make a choice. Spiritual maturity isn't a matter of talk but of power (1 Corinthians 4:20).

Encouragement and Prayer

But encourage one another daily, as long as it is called Today, so that none of you may be hardened by sin's deceitfulness. ~HEBREWS 3:13 NIV

(ALSO SEE HEBREWS 10:25; 1 THESSALONIANS 5:11)

Encouragement—just hearing that word seems to bring it!

It has been said that we need to receive at least seven positive remarks to overpower one negative comment. If you're having trouble believing that, just suppose it's time for a haircut and you decide you want something new. You give your stylist the thumbs up and the next day you meet your friends for breakfast to show it off. One after another they say, "Hey, that looks great, that really suits you!" But then you leave and go to work and one of your colleagues says, "What on earth were you thinking?"

Which one are you most prone to listen to? Even after all the positive comments, one bomb dropped can rock your boat and toss you into doubt about your decision to step out and try something new. Words are powerful.

The tongue has the power of life and death, and those who love it will eat its fruit. ~PROVERBS 18:21

We are created in the image of God. He created the world and everything in it by speaking words, and we have that creative ability as well. We get to choose what we want and don't want in our lives by the words we speak. We can speak life or death; it's our prerogative.

The tongue that brings healing is a tree of life, but a deceitful tongue crushes the spirit. ~PROVERBS 15:4

Reckless words pierce like a sword, but the tongue of the wise brings healing. ~PROVERBS 12:18

Words are powerful, and in the day in which we live, we hear more than enough negative remarks. What we need are words of life, words of encouragement. That is where we (Christians) come in. We have the ability to speak life to anybody and everybody that we come into contact with. It may not come naturally to us at first, but with practice and awareness of the power we have, we can become life—salt and light—in every situation we enter.

Now, when I say this doesn't come natural at first, I'm referring to the tendency of our flesh to want things its own way. ("Flesh" is a term for the greedy, selfish fallen human nature.). We train it, breaking off its sinful ways, by soaking in the Word of God and spending time in prayer, not only for ourselves but also for those in our circle of influence. If we don't stay deep in the Word and in prayer, we are fruitless.

I am the Vine; you are the branches. Whoever lives in Me and I in him bears much (abundant) fruit. However,

*apart from Me [cut off from vital union with Me] you can
do nothing.* ~JOHN 15:5 AMP

*When you bear (produce) much fruit, My Father is
honored and glorified, and you show and prove
yourselves to be true followers of Mine.* ~JOHN 15:8

We need to stay filled up on the Word and in prayer if
we want to use this powerful weapon called the tongue.

*So Jesus said to those Jews who had believed in Him, If
you abide in My word [hold fast to My teachings and live
in accordance with them], you are truly My disciples.*
~JOHN 8:31 AMP

When we take the time every day to read God's Word
and to pray it back to him, allowing the Holy Spirit to guide
us, speaking encouraging words isn't going to be a
hardship. The life we receive by daily renewing our minds
will naturally flow out from us, pouring the love God has
showered on us to others.

When we speak God's Word, we speak truth. When
truth is spoken, freedom enters. When freedom is seen,
encouragement flourishes.

Our tendency as Christians when people tell us what has
been going on in their lives is to end the conversation with,
"I'll pray for you." Of course, this is a great idea, but often
that's right where it stays: merely a pleasant parting
sentiment.

Prayer and encouragement go hand in hand. When we
spend time with our God—reading his Word, allowing his
Holy Spirit to guide our thoughts and talking to him about
what we have just read and how we could possibly apply it
to our life's situations—we walk away charged up and ready

to face whatever the world has to throw at us. And when we are daily charged-up, read-up and prayed-up, we cannot but help speak words of encouragement to those around us. There is no way we can contain the joy and peace we receive in the daily renewing of our minds when our heart, thoughts and plans are washed with the Word of God. The way to let it out is to speak that good Word to those around us.

Speaking God's Word brings refreshing and strength. For instance, just telling a person, "Oh, it'll be okay. You'll get through this," is not really a lot of help. But when you speak God's Word, you tell them that they are more than conquerors in Christ (Romans 8:37), reminding them that they can do all things through Christ (Philippians 4:13) and they have been given power and authority to trample on the enemy (Luke 10:19). Open up God's Word to them, showing them the solid foundation that they can build their life on. Show them that life is found in no one else but Jesus. (John 14:6; Acts 4:12).

My son, pay attention to what I say; listen closely to my words. Do not let them out of your sight, keep them within your heart; for they are life to those who find them and health to a man's whole body. ~Proverbs 4:20–22

The next time you want to say, "I'll pray for you," tell the person what you are going to pray and which Scripture(s) you are going to stand on for them on their behalf. That brings encouragement that is followed by confidence in God's Word, and the individual can then go on their own accord to drink from the spring of living water (John 7:38).

A generous man will prosper; he who refreshes others will himself be refreshed. ~PROVERBS 11:25

What is very unique about encouraging others is that when we speak words of life to build them up, fanning that spark into a flame, we get warmed as well (Luke 6:38, Proverbs 11:25). When we share and give of what has been given to us, it completes the circuit to fullness and wholeness.

As you go into your day, speak encouraging words to all you meet. The person who is packing your groceries or the person serving you coffee or the mechanic that's servicing your car—to whomever and wherever, be generous with compliments.

Give, and it will be given to you. A good measure, pressed down, shaken together and running over, will be poured into your lap. For with the measure you use, it will be measured to you. ~LUKE 6:38

When we are prayed up and sensitive to the Holy Spirit's leading, in order to make that circle of joy complete, we need to give it away. When we minister out of fullness, giving away compliments and encouragements is not a stretch in any way; it's just the overflow. Even in that, the more we give away of what God has shown us, the more there is. We cannot out-give God!

As you head into your day, look for ways to encourage those you come into contact with.

Be generous in your giving of compliments. Encouragement bounces back to you when you are open-handed with it to others.

The Lord bless you and keep you; the Lord make his face shine upon you and be gracious to you; the Lord

turn his face toward you and give you peace. ~NUMBERS
6:24–26

Rear-view Mirror

The invention of the rear-view mirror, I'm sure, was an important breakthrough, especially for those drivers who had a tough time turning their heads to see what, if anything, was coming up behind them. Today, in every car or truck or SUV that's made, a rear-view mirror is standard issue. It has to be there. If the mirror is used in the right way, driving is not only more fun, it is also a whole lot safer.

Some people, however, choose not to use it. Some drivers turn in and out of lanes without even a glance. They just don't seem to care—they are focused on the single task that they have set out to do and that seems to keep them locked in and unable to see other options.

On the other end of the spectrum, however, you have drivers who constantly keep looking back in their mirror. They spend little time watching what is in front of them, seemingly overly consumed with what's going on behind them.

Life is a lot like that. Some of us keep looking back to what was, hanging on to days gone by, hurts that happened and words that were spoken in anger, and we spend little time looking forward to see where we are steering. Others of us spend no time at all reflecting on what was. Errors that were made in the past are not learned from because we refuse to glance back.

I am not saying we should keep re-living the past; however, we do need to remember where we came from to see how far we've come. Many times we can become complacent with our lives, thinking we're just at a standstill, not moving forward. A glance to what used to be can often reveal the progress we have made.

Let me clarify this one more time: I'm not saying to live in the past. What's gone is gone, and there is nothing you can do to change what happened. You may not be where you would like to be, but, thank God, you are not where you were!

Forget the past! I know we all have those around us, even those who call themselves our friends, who dig up dirt from the past. Sometimes it's just to toss it in the air and watch where it lands. Other times they throw it in your face as if to discourage you from believing you are ever going to outlive or outgrow your follies. It might be intentional, or the person may not even know what they are doing. Either way, if you are a born again child of God, you need to listen to what he says. The God of all creation, the beginning and the end, has only one thing to say about your past:

"What Past?"

For as high as the heavens are above the earth, so great is his love for those who fear him; as far as the east is from the west, so far has he removed our transgressions from us. ~PSALM 103:11–12

When we come to God through Jesus Christ, he separates us from our sins, cleans us up (1 John 1:9) and forgets them, giving us a fresh start with no condemnation, no "I remember what you did" accusations tied to it.

*For [the Spirit which] you have now received [is] not a
spirit of slavery to put you once more in bondage to fear,
but you have received the Spirit of adoption [the Spirit
producing sonship] in [the bliss of] which we cry, Abba
(Father)! Father! ~ROMANS 8:15 AMP*

"Abba" means "Daddy." We can come to God as
children of our "daddy"—our heavenly Father. Some
earthly fathers are unloving, absent or even abusive and
hurtful. However, that's not the kind of daddy my God is;
he is accepting, wanting me to come to him when I am
feeling weak, hurt or beat up by the words that are spoken
against me.

God has the final say. When God says you are forgiven,
that you are righteous and you are his chosen one, who
does anyone else think they are to say, "No—God is wrong;
it is my opinion that counts"? Secondly, why on earth
would you take the time to listen to those worthless
opinions in the first place?

When you give your life to Jesus, making him your
Lord and Saviour, he makes you a new creation, something
that did not exist here before. The old you is gone and the
new you has come. I am not just making this up—it is in
God's Word:

*Therefore if any person is [ingrafted] in Christ (the
Messiah) he is a new creation (a new creature
altogether); the old [previous moral and spiritual condition]
has passed away. Behold, the fresh and new has come!
But all things are from God, Who through Jesus Christ
reconciled us to Himself [received us into favor, brought
us into harmony with Himself] and gave to us the ministry
of reconciliation [that by word and deed we might aim to
bring others into harmony with Him]. ~2 CORINTHIANS 5:17–18 AMP*

If you don't see yourself the way God sees you, then you will more than likely see yourself the way you think others see you. That kind of thinking brings along with it a whole list of traps and snares and weights that hold you back from moving forward. It becomes a downward spiral where one poor choice makes way for the next.

But there is good news: you can stop that downward spiral in your life today—now!

The Bible talks about forgetting what is behind. What has happened in the past is exactly that—PAST. Leave it there!

I, even I, am he who blots out your transgressions, for my own sake, and remembers your sins no more. ~ISAIAH 43:25

Bless (affectionately, gratefully praise) the Lord, O my soul, and forget not [one of] all His benefits—Who forgives [every one of] all your iniquities, Who heals [each one of] all your diseases . . . ~PSALM 103:3 AMP

I do not consider, brethren, that I have captured and made it my own [yet]; but one thing I do [it is my one aspiration]: forgetting what lies behind and straining forward to what lies ahead, I press on toward the goal to win the [supreme and heavenly] prize to which God in Christ Jesus is calling us upward. ~PHILIPPIANS 3:13–14 AMP

I sought (inquired of) the Lord and required Him [of necessity and on the authority of His Word], and He heard me, and delivered me from all my fears. They looked to Him and were radiant; their faces shall never blush for shame or be confused. This poor man cried, and the Lord heard him, and saved him out of all his troubles. The Angel of the Lord encamps around those who fear Him [who revere and worship Him with awe] and each of them He delivers. O taste and see that the

Lord [our God] is good! Blessed (happy, fortunate, to be envied) is the man who trusts and takes refuge in Him.
~*Psalm 34:4–8 AMP*

Your best days are not behind you, they are in front of you. May God be true, and every man a liar! (Romans 3:4) Don't give up!

Duck Pond

Spring is a great time of year. The first signs of geese flying overhead seems to indicate that all is well, we are past the cold bite of winter and the warm days of spring are within reach.

Last fall when the geese and ducks were preparing to head south for the winter, I went to a duck pond in one of the parks to see the hundreds of birds floating, fighting, quacking and preening themselves. Some of the people who were at the water's edge had bags of seed to feed the birds.

The next day I returned with a bag of "wild bird" seed. It contained small seeds and other grains, some ground almost to a fine power. As I approached the pond, the geese took notice of me and started honking and quacking and coming out of the water to greet me. Since the seeds were so small and so much of it ground so fine, I thought the best thing to do would be to put it out on the walkway so they could pick it up. Some of the geese did, but for the most part, they walked past it. I thought maybe they were full already and not interested in that type of food.

Then I realized that the hard, uneven surface was preventing them from picking up the feed. So I walked to the water's edge and dropped a few handfuls in the grass.

Suddenly a group of birds began bumping and pushing each other to get to the seeds. Geese from the pond swam over to the area as if waiting in line for their turn.

Just to see what would happen, I tossed a large handful of seeds into the pond. The birds went into a frenzied feast. At first I was shocked by their ability to eat almost dust-fine seeds from water. But then I remembered that they were geese.

So what's with all this wild bird feeding stuff? What I learned from this was that in handling the gospel of Jesus Christ we need to understand where people are when we are talking to them.

Sometimes people simply walk away from God's Word because they do not understand how to eat (how to accept and apply) what is being offered. When I put the seed on the sidewalk, the geese barely ate any. They are not accustomed to eating off asphalt and concrete or finding a food source there. It made perfect sense to me, but not them. But when I dropped the seeds into the grass, more birds came and ate. They are used to clipping through grass with their tweezer-tipped beaks to pick up bits of seed.

The handful of seed that was scattered over the water was a no contest. That is their playing field, what they understand, where they live—they are comfortable and feel safe in the water. Giving them what they understood where they were at was the best way to feed the birds.

People sometimes seem resistant and many times walk away when we want to share Jesus with them, and I wonder if it's due to the fact that we are trying to feed them something in a way they are not familiar with. We know we have good food (John 6:35), we know that God is good and that Jesus is the only way (John. 14:6; Acts 4:12); however, if we do not share that good news with the people in a way they can understand, the truth we hold out is no truth to them at all. The Word needs to be presented in such a way that the person you are sharing it with feels safe, comfortable and able to accept (eat) what is being offered.

When I came towards the duck pond, geese and ducks alike came out of the water towards me. They must have seen the bag I was carrying. Maybe through conditioning they assume that when a human comes to "their" pond they have something that will benefit them.

If you identify yourself as a born again Christian and carry the same concern as Jesus did for the lost, then when you enter someone's space you are carrying something that will benefit them. But don't just toss it in front of them any which way and expect them to figure it out.

Study and be eager and do your utmost to present yourself to God approved (tested by trial), a workman who has no cause to be ashamed, correctly analyzing and accurately dividing [rightly handling and skillfully teaching] the Word of Truth. ~2 TIMOTHY 2:15 AMP

Be a person who satisfies hungry expectation with good seed.

Slap to the Head

Before I go any further, I should explain that I'm not talking about violence here. Sometimes we all, whether for real or just verbally, need a "slap" to startle us out of the narrow tunnel vision we can get caught up in when we look at circumstances in our lives. We often say, "Give your head a shake!" meaning, "Come on, friend, you're not assessing the situation in the correct way!"

(Okay, with that cleared up, back to the slap).

In my experience, there are at least two different kinds of "slaps," one from an "outside" source, and the other, self-inflicted. The slap from outside is generally applied to the back of the head—not very hard, just swift enough to get you to pay attention. The single-handed slap is self-administered, palm facing you as you kind of "pound" it against your forehead, saying, "What on earth was I thinking?"

More times than not, we need a "slap to the head." It's like we forget what the Bible has told us, and when we slip up we carry the guilt around like a heavy fur coat, wearing the condemnation that the devil is tossing at us.

So, here's one for the back of the head just in case you are in that very position. If you are not in that spot, then use this as a reminder to not step into that snare. Let's look at 1 John 5:18–20.

> *We know that anyone born of God does not continue to sin; the one who was born of God keeps him safe, and the evil one cannot harm him. We know that we are children of God, and that the whole world is under the control of the evil one. We know also that the Son of God has come and has given us understanding, so that we may know him who is true. And we are in him who is true—even in his Son Jesus Christ. He is the true God and eternal life.*

You may be saying to yourself, "Of course I sin." And you're right—we all make mistakes. James 3:2 confirms this: "*We all stumble in many ways.*"

Sin means to miss the mark. If you are going about your day and you are doing all you know to do to live your life for Jesus but you blow it—did you miss the mark? Yep! Sure did. But it wasn't intentional. You didn't plan to stumble; it just happened in the events of the day. Confess that sin to God and move on (1 John 1:9).

What about when you wilfully sin, though? Going against what you know is completely wrong, ignoring God's Word and his will for your life and choosing to go your way instead seems different than merely missing the mark.

It is God's kindness that leads us to repentance (Romans 2:4), and either way, sin confessed to God is taken care of, forgotten. Jesus will keep you safe from the condemnation the devil likes to throw on you and try to convince you to wear. Focusing on the Word of God and knowing that his Holy Spirit is here to lead you and to guide you will block out the accuser's voice and allow you to walk in the forgiveness of God as you renew your decision to follow him more closely.

> *This then is how we know that we belong to the truth, and how we set our hearts at rest in his presence whenever our hearts condemn us. For God is greater than our hearts, and he knows everything. ~1 JOHN 3:19–20*

1 John 5:19 goes on to say,

> *We know that we are children of God, and that the whole world is under the control of the evil one.*

(Here comes the single-handed "What was I thinking?" slap.)

The last verse above says, "*We know...*" but do YOU know you are God's child?

If somewhere along the line you have been led to believe that you are not God's child, there is a 100% chance that you are not going to act like one of his chosen. It also pretty much guarantees that you aren't going to turn to him in your time of need or times of worship.

> *I took you from the ends of the earth, from its farthest corners I called you. I said, 'You are my servant'; I have chosen you and have not rejected you. ~ISAIAH 41:9*
>
> *How great is the love the Father has lavished on us, that we should be called children of God! And that is what we are! ~1 JOHN 3:1*

Listen, God chose you and he set a plan in place for your life (Jeremiah 29:11). No matter what anyone has said about you or your future, you are the only one who can do the tasks that God has planned out for your life. No one else can take your place. You are precious to God, he hears your prayers, he see your tears, he knows your joy.

NO ONE can stop you from accomplishing the plan God has for your life except you. Choosing to give up and walk away is the only thing that is going to stop you from carrying out God's amazing destiny for you. If you have accepted Jesus as your personal Lord and Saviour, you are God's child. Do not ever forget that!

> *We know also that the Son of God has come and has given us understanding, so that we may know him who is true. And we are in him who is true—even in his Son Jesus Christ. He is the true God and eternal life.* ~1 JOHN 5:20

God has given us understanding. When we ask Jesus into our lives we are also given the promised Holy Spirit. He leads us into all truth (John 14:26), gives life to our bodies (Romans 8:11) and acts as a seal, a deposit and guarantee of what is to come (2 Corinthians 1:22).

The Bible should be not only read daily but also thought about and thought through. The Word of God is living and active (Hebrews 4:12), not just a book with words in it. When you take the Word and absorb it by reading it, praying it, speaking it and putting it into action, understanding will be one of the many benefits.

Three times in these three verses we hear the same thing—"*We know...*" (v. 18), "*We know...*" (v. 19), "*We know...*" (v. 20).

(SMACK) - Get the idea?

It's All Good

And we know that in all things God works for the good of those who love him, who have been called according to his purpose. ~ROMANS 8:28

In all things... What "things"? The "not so good things" of life. There isn't anybody on the face of this earth that hasn't come through a tough situation.

Everybody has been hurt by somebody. The strange thing is that we usually feel we are the only ones going through what we are going through. We want the world to stop and see how tough it is for us and how badly we have been wounded. Yes, stuff happens, but we cannot continue to live well with hurt and pain. We have to find a way to move on, and that takes forgiveness, no matter how great the offence.

There are times when people get confused, using the above verse to prove that God brought the tragedy on them, but of course that is not in any way what the verse implies.

"All things work together" doesn't mean God is happy when you hit rough waters in life. It means that if you don't take your eyes off Jesus (Hebrews 12:2) to look at what is going on around you, he will use whatever is going on to

move you forward. We can trust more in Christ and his Word than in what we see with our eyes.

These "things" can be used as stepping stones up to the next level. Not every bad thing that happens in life is caused by the devil. Some things are self-inflicted. Some things are done when we don't think about what we're doing. Some things are just life! The recipe of life includes some "not so good things," so we have to train ourselves to keep our eyes on Jesus and on what he says, not on our circumstances and what they seem to be telling us (2 Corinthians 5:7).

. . . IN ALL THINGS GOD WORKS . . .

Many people complain that they want God to speak to them, they want to see him at work. The sad thing is that God IS working—he IS speaking to them, but they often aren't taking the time to listen. When we are faced with problems that seem to have no way around or through, we can be assured that "God works." When all looks hopeless and lost and you are asking yourself "What good is this? What's the point?" know that God is well aware of the situation and fully capable and very willing to trade your ashes for beauty, your loss for gain, your pain for hope and your tears of sorrow for tears of joy.

. . . GOD WORKS . . . FOR GOOD . . .

Look for and aim at praying and believing for good! Take the time to listen and let God guide you towards his good and perfect will (Romans 12:2). The devil works for your destruction—God works for your good. You cast the deciding vote!

In all these things we are more than conquerors through him who loved us. ~ROMANS 12:37

Have you ever tasted 90% cocoa chocolate? It's pretty bitter. Most people don't like it because they are used to milk chocolate that has a comparatively low proportion of cocoa in it. Life at times can be pretty bitter as well. Most of us have been in tough bitter spots when gagging it down wasn't a fun or simple task. Most of us just want the "*Milk Chocolate*" life—smooth and easy to take, but life just isn't that way.

Life has its twists and turns, so how are we supposed to handle it?

To them God has chosen to make known among the Gentiles the glorious riches of this mystery, which is Christ in you, the hope of glory. ~COLOSSIANS 1:27

Jesus defeated and made a spectacle of Satan on the cross; he beat the devil hands down. Because you are in Christ Jesus you share in that victory. Jesus won the battle once and for all and we are in him, so *we are conquerors in everything, no matter what comes our way.* The only thing that stops us from taking our rightful place with Jesus is our attitude and limited understanding of how God is on our side and that no matter what happens, we WIN. We can stand firm, no matter how hard the storm rages around us.

Romans 8:28–30 in *The Message* translation reads this way:

That's why we can be so sure that every detail in our lives of love for God is worked into something good. God knew what he was doing from the very beginning. He decided from the outset to shape the lives of those who love him along the same lines as the life of his Son. The Son stands first in the line of humanity he restored. We see the original and intended shape of our lives there in him. After God made that decision of what his children should be like, he followed it up by calling people by name. After he called them by name, he set them on a solid basis with himself. And then, after getting them established, he stayed with them to the end, gloriously completing what he had begun. ~MSG

That's so good! Tough times are coming, and some of us have already tasted the bitterness of hard circumstances. To get through those times we need to have the "roots" of our faith deeply planted in God's Word, knowing it well, so that when the enemy comes up with his lies and stories we can stand firm with the truth and run him out and beat him up every time.

It's all good!

You are blessed, Saint! God is good; his love endures forever!

What My Dentist Taught Me

I am blessed to not only have a Christian for a dentist, but one who is passionate about his service to Jesus Christ not only in his speech but in his actions. Going to the dentist used to be something I dreaded. Now it's an appointment I look forward to because I know God is guiding my dentist's hands and God's plan for both our lives is to prosper us, so no bad thing can happen! (What a joy!)

I went in for some dental work a while ago, and to help me understand what was going on in my mouth, my dentist took the time to draw out a detailed picture of a tooth for me. He explained the process of how germs get into a tooth, which causes decay and the eventual downfall of the tooth. During that conversation I thought about how much

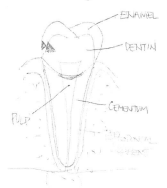

similar the Christian life is to that tooth.

The outer part of the tooth is covered in a very hard substance called "enamel," and underneath that layer is the "dentin." That's all above the gum line. Below the gum line you have the "periodontal ligament" that goes around the perimeter of the tooth, further in is the "cementum," and at the centre of the tooth is the "pulp."

My tooth looked good from the outside. I didn't realize I had a problem until the X-ray showed us the inside of the tooth. I had a small "hole" that went through the enamel and the dentin and was allowing germs into the inside of the tooth. That is where the decay was taking place. But like I said, from the outside I couldn't see anything was wrong. Actually, I thought everything was just swell.

And that is when I thought about my Christian walk.

We have an enemy of our souls who is out to steal from us, kill us and destroy anything we put our hands to (John 10:10). We are not unaware of the devil's schemes (2 Corinthians 2:11), or at least we don't have to be. For many years he's been fooling people, deceiving them and pushing them off course with his lies. We need to be aware!

I was oblivious about what was going on in my own mouth. Nothing seemed wrong until I had an X-ray taken of the tooth to see what on earth was going on under the guise of "all is well."

Now, if I would have allowed my emotions to take over (the "fear" of going to the dentist's office to get the tooth looked at), the decay would have won out, even with the tooth looking good on the outside. We are all emotional beings, but just because we have emotions doesn't mean they should "have" us!

Do not allow the discomfort of examining your spiritual life to keep you from probing your devotional time—How is the time being spent? How much time is really being put into it? What application is coming from that time? We can get so used to doing what we do, taking life, breath and even health so much for granted, that we simply carry on from day to day, slowly drawing further and further away from the life-giving Word of God.

Busy schedules, late nights, early mornings—excuses are not hard to come by. We attend church at least once a week, many times twice, we listen to teaching CDs from time to time (well maybe not that often), and we feel good about life and where we are at. Suddenly something comes up and we're not sure what to do. That's about the time we begin to understand that the Word isn't just to be stored in the mind; it needs to be daily coming out of the mouth in application.

When we get lazy in our study and use of God's Word, we allow it to slip into a void. That separation is like the small chip in my tooth, allowing weakness to slowly erode the centre while the surface appears to be in good shape.

A little sleep, a little slumber, a little folding of the hands to rest—and poverty will come on you like a bandit and scarcity like an armed man. ~PROVERBS 6:10–11

I use this verse as an illustration for spiritual poverty. When we start getting slack in areas of our devotional life, we feel we still know the Word but it's not coming out of our mouth or filling our thoughts and actions and re-actions. We are slowly getting robbed.

The enemy isn't going to come charging into your house and scream at you to stop reading the Word of God. He won't tell you that when you speak God's Word and live by it, it terrifies him and makes it impossible for him to get his hooks into you. No way! He will come at you in a much more subtle and deceptive way.

We tend to get complacent fairly quickly. What was new and awe-inspiring a short time ago is now "just there."

It's kind of like the "you can't see the forest for the trees" idea. After growing accustomed to secure homes, nutritious food and clean drinking water or the nearness of friends and family who protect and support us, we no longer recognize how blessed we are to have them in our lives.

Make every effort to prevent this in your life. Test yourself—are you doing what you "say" or "think" you are doing? If everybody in the church was doing "as well" as you are, would the church still be in operation?

Examine yourselves to see whether you are in the faith; test yourselves. Do you not realize that Christ Jesus is in you—unless, of course, you fail the test? ~2 CORINTHIANS 13:5

I had no idea that my tooth was failing until a deep inspection was done. It was just a little chip—"No big deal," I thought—but destruction was underway. How could I have prevented it from happening in the first place? I could have avoided that whole incident by brushing my teeth regularly and flossing properly.

Admittedly, there are times when it just isn't possible to brush your teeth, like when you are out for dinner and then the conversation moves over to the coffee shop. You're stuck with the sweets you had at the restaurant still interlaced in your teeth. But that's where the similarities between teeth and the Christian life stop. There is always an opportunity to refresh yourself in the Word or spend time with the Lord in worship and praise him. The list is endless: when you are at work, driving, shopping, standing in line at the check out . . . You don't need a toothbrush, floss and a sink to spit into; praising God isn't confined to the bathroom like brushing your teeth is.

I encourage you to take a look at yourself. Ask God to show you what is standing between you and him that is allowing decay to set in.

(For further reading, see Psalm 33:5; 89:1; Matthew 28:18–20; 1 Corinthians 1:9; 2 Thessalonians 3:3; Hebrews 10:23; 13:5, 8.)

Friends with God?

It's not only possible to be a friend of God, it is his will, his desire, to call you friend.

We were all lost in sin, and sin separates us from God. When Jesus went to the cross (John 3:16) and gave his life for ours, he traded places with us. We got his righteousness—he got our sin, shame and sicknesses. He took the curse for us.

> So from now on we regard no one from a worldly point of view. Though we once regarded Christ in this way, we do so no longer. Therefore, if anyone is in Christ, he is a new creation; the old has gone, the new has come!
> ~2 CORINTHIANS 5:16–17

> Christ redeemed us from the curse of the law by becoming a curse for us, for it is written: "Cursed is everyone who is hung on a tree." ~GALATIANS 3:13

Jesus became the curse that we were so that now God sees us through Jesus, who made us righteous. The sin account that we'd racked up is now wiped out, paid in full and forgotten by God.

How do you get to be friends with God? First you give your life to him. When Jesus Christ comes into your life (at your invitation), you become something new; you become a New You, different from who you were before.

> *Therefore if any person is [ingrafted] in Christ (the Messiah) he is a new creation (a new creature altogether); the old [previous moral and spiritual condition] has passed away. Behold, the fresh and new has come!* ~2 CORINTHIANS 5:17 AMP

Just like you need to keep in touch with your friends by hanging out with them, texting them, calling them, etc., you need to hang out with God. Spending time with God isn't something that has to be done for a set amount of time in a certain location on a certain day. You can spend time with God anytime.

Some think that prayer can only be done on your knees in church or in your room, but prayer can be done all day, no matter where you're at. Thank God for his goodness and faithfulness. Thank God for your food, for the great weather, for anything and everything. You can keep on talking to God as you go to work, while you're there and on your way home.

God wants to spend time with you too; he is interested in everything you do. Make time to talk to him. Learn how to listen for what he is saying to you.

When you are talking to God, be candid. You don't have to make things sound great. God knows everything, so there is no point in trying to cover up what he already knows. Be honest and open with God in your conversations.

When you spend time with your friends, you learn to trust them, and God is even more that way—he will never let you down! (Hebrews 13:5) Learn to trust God and lean on him and his Word.

You are my friends if you do what I command. ~JOHN 15:14

We don't obey God because we have to or fear not to, we obey God because we trust him and love him.

As the Father has loved me, so have I loved you. Now remain in my love. If you obey my commands, you will remain in my love, just as I have obeyed my Father's commands and remain in his love. I have told you this so that my joy may be in you and that your joy may be complete. ~JOHN 15:9–11

Being God's friend takes focus. Friends care about what their friends care about and God cares about people. He loves people so much that he sent Jesus to this earth to die a sinner's death just so he could redeem you and me from hell—so he could be our God, our friend.

Now that I am God's friend, I care enough about the ones he loves to pass this good news on. I don't want anybody to live without hope, thinking that living for ourselves is as good as it gets. I don't want people to die in their sin and then spend eternity in hell, and neither does God. Friends care about what friends care about, and that takes focus.

Being God's friend requires you to get hungry—not for food, but for the things of God. To want God more than anything else in your life. To be willing to set down your ideas and your dreams and go after God's will for your life.

One thing I ask of the Lord, this is what I seek: that I may dwell in the house of the Lord all the days of my life, to gaze upon the beauty of the Lord and to seek him in his temple. ~PSALM 27:4

Because your love is better than life, my lips will glorify you. ~PSALM 63:3

Being a friend of God is better than life itself! He knows the plans he has for our lives, and no matter what happens, he can turn what the devil means for bad in our lives into good. But we can't be jumping back and forth, saying, "I trust God," one day and then, when it seems like the bottom falls out, starting to doubt, going back to calling things the way we think we see them.

Being friends with God cannot truly be compared to the friendships we have here on earth. Our friends may make mistakes and bad calls and say things they don't really mean. Hurt people hurt people—really, our friends are much like us.

God's friendship with us is perfect from his side; we are the ones who mess up. We are the ones who call him down when we think a situation should have gone a different way. We are the ones who caused him to sacrifice his Son on a cross to die a horrible death to get us back into friendship with him.

Through all this, God still waits for you to talk to him, to invite him into your life.

Jesus longs to help you and heal you; you just need to call him up.

I've Got the Power!

How many times have you heard people say, "I feel powerless in this situation"? Even worse, how many times have you heard yourself say that?

Powerlessness comes from doubt. As soon as you doubt God's Word, you start the journey to feeling you have no power to do anything about the situation you are in. But we have been given power:

> *I have given you authority to trample on snakes and scorpions and to overcome all the power of the enemy; nothing will harm you.* ~LUKE 10:19

How much "harm" is left to get at us when God tells us, "Nothing will harm you?" Exactly how much is "all" power—is there anything missing? (Let me help you: "'No, nothing is missing!") Jesus Christ did not come into this world to give us just a "little bit" of life or just a "glimpse" of how good he is; Jesus came to give us life, and that to the FULL! (John 10:10b).

Sure, when we get to heaven we are going to see far more clearly who Jesus is and what he has done for us (1 Corinthians 13:12), but for now we are to be living life to the full, not limping around feeling powerless. He has given us everything we need for a life of godliness (2 Peter 1:3). You have the power! It's right there in that dark little cave under your nose. It's called the "tongue."

In Revelation chapter one, John hears a voice telling him to write down what he sees. When he turns to see where the voice is coming from, he sees someone "like the son of man" (Jesus) and he begins to describe him.

> *In his right hand he held seven stars, and out of his mouth came a sharp double-edged sword. His face was like the sun shining in all its brilliance.* ~REVELATION 1:16

He said he saw a "double edged sword" coming out of his mouth. Now, where have we heard that term before?

> *For the Word of God is living and active. Sharper than any double-edged sword, it penetrates even to dividing soul and spirit, joints and marrow; it judges the thoughts and attitudes of the heart.* ~HEBREWS 4:12

Jesus was speaking the Word. Now go from the last book of the Bible to the first book and take a look at Genesis. In the first chapter we see the phrase "and God said" at least six times! When God spoke, things were created, they came into being. Stuff happens when God's Word is spoken!

> *So God created man in his own image, in the image of God he created him; male and female he created them.*
> ~GENESIS 1:27

If God's power is in his spoken Word, then we, who are created in his image, also have the ability to speak things into existence. God's Word backs this up:

*The tongue has the power of life and death, and those
who love it will eat its fruit.* ~PROVERBS 18:21

You can predict your future; just listen to what you are
saying now. Keep on saying you are never going to make it,
that you don't think you have what it takes and things like
that, and you are going to get what you say—failure, and a
bumper crop of it! On the other hand, when you speak life
to yourself, your friends, your job and the situations you
face, then you will get a bumper crop of the blessings you
sow.

You are not powerless!
You are a child of the Most High God!
You are created in his image!
You were not designed to fail!

Start calling in the blessings that are yours in Christ.
Stop cutting them off and setting up road blocks with what
you say. Open the floodgates by confessing God's Word. If
you need some help to "prime the pump," here is a list of
promises to start you off:

- *This is the day the Lord has made, and I will rejoice
  and be glad in it.*

- *God's mercy and grace are new every morning in
  my life (Lamentations 3:22–23).*

- *I am God's child (1 John 3:1).*

- *I have been filled with His Spirit (2 Corinthians
  1:22).*

- *My steps are ordered and directed by God (Psalm
  139:16; Proverbs 4:11).*

- *I am the head and not the tail (Deuteronomy 28:13).*

- *I am above and not below.*

- *I am blessed coming in and blessed going out (Deuteronomy 28:6).*

- *I am ready for anything and equal to anything through Christ Jesus. He always causes me to win (2 Corinthians 2:14).*

- *No weapon formed against me will prosper (Isaiah 54:17).*

- *I am strong in the Lord and the power of His might (Ephesians 6:10).*

Keep your eyes on Jesus! (Hebrews12:2–3). You are NOT powerless—YOU HAVE THE POWER!

What Does God Think of Me?
Titus 3:1–8

D o you ever wonder what people think about you? Do you even care?

A lot of people live their lives trying to please people, worried about what they think others are thinking about them. But have you ever stopped yourself to think about what God thinks about you? Has it even crossed your mind that you are important enough to God that he'd take time to give you his attention?

Well, he does. You are not just a face in the crowd.

Paul wanted to remind Titus and his church who they were in Jesus, what they had in Jesus, what God had done in them through Jesus and what God expected of them as believers in Jesus. What he wrote in his letter has a lot to say to us as well:

1. God thinks you are worth the price he paid for you.

He loves you way more than you can get your mind around (1 Corinthians 2:9).

At one time we too were foolish, disobedient, deceived and enslaved by all kinds of passions and pleasures. We lived in malice and envy, being hated and hating one another. ~TITUS 3:3

There is no denying what we were like before we met Jesus: foolish, disobedient, deceived, envious and hateful. We were in pretty rough shape (Ephesians 2:1–3; 1 Corinthians 6:9–10).

Even when we were messed up and doing everything God didn't want us to be doing, he still loved us (Jeremiah 31:3). He could have just let us go and get what we deserve, but he chose to show us his love.

But when the kindness and love of God our Savior appeared, he saved us, not because of righteous things we had done, but because of his mercy. . . . through Jesus Christ our Savior. ~TITUS 3:4, 6B

God showed us his love by sending Jesus to take the punishment for us (Romans 5:6–8; John 3:16; 1 John 4:9–10; 2 Corinthians 5:21).

. . .he saved us, not because of righteous things we had done, but because of his mercy. He saved us through the washing of rebirth and renewal by the Holy Spirit, whom he poured out on us generously through Jesus Christ our Savior. ~TITUS 3:5–6

God sees us exactly as we really are, and he loves us anyway.

2. You are in the right place.

. . . so that, having been justified by his grace . . . ~TITUS 3:7A

When we are justified by God, all record of our sin is wiped from his memory. Think of it this way: "Just-as-if-I'd" never sinned (Jeremiah 31:34; Hebrews 8:12; 10:16–17).

> . . . *we might become heirs having the hope of eternal life* . . . *~TITUS 3:7B*

- *Jesus is always with me. (Hebrews 13:5; Matthew 28:20)*

- *Jesus has promised that all my needs will be met. (Philippians 4:19; Matthew 6:25–34)*

- *Jesus cares and knows about what's going on in my life. (Hebrews 4:15)*

- *Jesus hears me when I pray. (Hebrews 4:16)*

Look at it from every angle—when we're living life in Christ, we've got it made. That's not just for now when we live here on this planet, but also in eternity. Jesus is preparing a home for us in heaven (John 14:1–3). We have reservations for the best (1 Peter 1:3–5), and we will never have to experience death or sorrow again (Revelation 21:4).

We have the best here and now and after this too! What a God we serve!

> *Know that the Lord is God. It is he who made us, and we are his; we are his people, the sheep of his pasture.* *~PSALM 100:3*

God saved you for a purpose and part of that purpose is to use you for his glory. Just the way you carry yourself from day to day speaks volumes to the world around you. Living your life in the joy and power the Lord has given you is a powerful witness (Matthew 5:16). He saved you to put you to work for him (Ephesians 2:10; 2 Corinthians 9:8; Colossians 1:10; James 2:18).

Do you want to see the power and provision of God? Then step out of the area in which you can control everything into the area where only God can get you through. That's where you will see his power at work.

Temptation
Romans 6:11–18

Temptation: an enticement or invitation to sin with the implied promise of greater good to be derived from following the way of disobedience.

How many temptations do we face in an ordinary day? It's nuts when you stop and think about it. At every turn and every decision, temptation lurks in the shadows, waiting for a mindless moment to get us to do, say or think something way off base. Many times people feel lost or hopeless because they felt the heat of temptation when they were "trying" so hard to live and walk the Christian life. Because they were "tempted," they concluded they had already committed the crime. Not so.

Here are a few points you should know about temptation:

1. Temptation is not a sin. It's giving in to the temptation that is wrong.

> . . . but each one is tempted when, by his own evil desire, he is dragged away and enticed. Then, after desire has conceived, it gives birth to sin; and sin, when it is full-grown, gives birth to death. ~JAMES 1:14–15

Just because a thought comes racing across your mind and attempts to drag you off course, it doesn't make you a failure. Temptation is just that: it's something that is trying to lure you away from your game plan. You can't stop a bird from flying over your head, but you can stop it from building a nest on it, so watch what you think about. Thoughts become imaginations, which then turn into actions.

2. Everybody runs into temptation.

No temptation has seized you except what is common to man . . . ~1 CORINTHIANS 10:13A

You are not the first person that has faced temptation, nor are you the last. It happens to the best of us and no one is immune to it. In fact, there are no temptations that you have faced that Jesus didn't first face. Every person that was used by God struggled; the question was not a matter of whether they would struggle but what they would do about it.

Stop for a minute here. Think about it. You're not alone in your struggle.

3. God does not tempt anyone.

When tempted, no one should say, "God is tempting me." For God cannot be tempted by evil, nor does he tempt anyone. ~JAMES 1:13

We cannot blame God for our temptation to sin. When we try to accomplish or obtain something with our own strength rather than through his provision, we start to feed a desire that leads us down the slippery road to sin.

4. There is a way out.

But when you are tempted, he will also provide a way out so that you can stand up under it. ~1 CORINTHIANS 10:13B

God never leaves us out on a limb by ourselves. He has given us his powerful Word and his Holy Spirit to lead us into all truth. The devil would like you to think you are all by yourself and that you have gone too far, you're hopeless and God doesn't want anything to do with you. But that is such a lie! The devil knows that when you understand and put into practice the way of escape, he and his lies are shown for what they are—all lies!

You need to know that you, as a redeemed child of God, are righteous in God's sight. (2 Corinthians 5:17, 21). You are his; God WILL NOT leave you!

If we have been united with him like this in his death, we will certainly also be united with him in his resurrection. For we know that our old self was crucified with him so that the body of sin might be done away with, that we should no longer be slaves to sin . . . Now if we died with Christ, we believe that we will also live with him. For we know that since Christ was raised from the dead, he cannot die again; death no longer has mastery over him. The death he died, he died to sin once for all; but the life he lives, he lives to God. In the same way, count yourselves dead to sin but alive to God in Christ Jesus. Therefore do not let sin reign in your mortal body so that you obey its evil desires. Do not offer the parts of your body to sin, as instruments of wickedness, but rather offer yourselves to God, as those who have been brought from death to life; and offer the parts of your body to him as instruments of righteousness. For sin

shall not be your master, because you are not under law,
but under grace. ~ROMANS 6:5–6, 8–14

Jesus makes it possible for us to say no to temptation. Why? Sin is now powerless because of the work done on the cross, Christ died for our sin, and we died with him in his death. He was our substitute, and likewise, we rose with him; Jesus' resurrection is ours.

When you give your life to Jesus, you get all this and more! You are no longer under the grip of sin! Before you gave your life to Jesus, you had no defence. You had to sin because that's all you knew; you didn't know any other way. But when you make Jesus your Lord and Saviour, you have a new owner. You get hooked up to a new power supply that gives you the ability to rise above sin and gives you the power to say no to it.

Let this truth take root in your life today—you have the resurrection power living in you! See temptation for what it is.

Walk on water, Saint! (Continued)

Temptation (Conclusion)
Matthew 4:1–11

Jesus beat Satan, hell, sin, death, temptation, sickness . . . the list goes on. Jesus won at the cross.

God has given us his Word, the Bible, a book of promises. When we not only study and read his Word but speak it over ourselves and our situations, family and friends—basically, when we have our hearts and our mouths filled with God's Word—we overcome anything and everything the enemy tries to toss at us.

God has placed his Holy Spirit in our hearts as a deposit guaranteeing what is to come (2 Corinthians 1:22), to give life to our mortal bodies (Romans 8:11) and to lead us into all truth (John 14:26). We are more than conquerors in Christ.

When temptation comes a-knockin' at the door . . .

1. Use God's Word. (Matthew 4)

Jesus was led by the Spirit into the desert to be tempted. Interestingly enough, this time of temptation came right after a powerful spiritual experience. Three times the devil tempted him and each time Jesus responded by saying, "It is written" and quoting God's Word (Matthew 4:7, 10).

When we are faced with temptation, the sure way to overcome it is by using the same method Jesus used. Speak God's Word—that's why it's so important to be reading it daily as well as memorizing it. When temptation sets a trap for you and you are caught up in it, you can speak the powerful Word of God to send the devil running!

2. Get away from temptation. (Genesis 39)

To get away from temptation you turn and run, physically and mentally. Consider what Joseph did when Potiphar's wife tried to seduce him. He said, "How could I do such a wicked thing and sin against God?" He ran from temptation—right out of the house! Do whatever it takes to not give in. Don't wait until the desire is in high gear before you take action against temptation! When you are faced with the temptation to think nasty thoughts, take those thoughts captive (2 Corinthians10:3–5) and get God's Word coming out of your mouth.

> *Fix your thoughts on what is true, and honorable, and right, and pure, and lovely, and admirable. Think about things that are excellent and worthy of praise. ~PHILIPPIANS 4:8 NLT*

3. Deal with temptation before it comes. (Proverbs 7)

Many times temptations come right out of the blue, but other times we set them up for ourselves; we sow the seed and help it grow from a thought into a full-blown movie in our mind. If you don't want to get burned, then don't play with fire.

Proverbs 7 tells the story of a young guy who gets entangled with an immoral woman. But the warning is not just about sexual temptation; it relates to anything that can take us down if we give in to it.

> At the window of my house I looked out through the lattice. I saw among the simple, I noticed among the young men, a youth who lacked judgment. He was going down the street near her corner, walking along in the direction of her house at twilight, as the day was fading, as the dark of night set in. Then out came a woman to meet him, dressed like a prostitute and with crafty intent. (She is loud and defiant, her feet never stay at home; now in the street, now in the squares, at every corner she lurks.) She took hold of him and kissed him . . . All at once he followed her like an ox going to the slaughter, like a deer stepping into a noose till an arrow pierces his liver, like a bird darting into a snare, little knowing it will cost him his life. ~PROVERBS 7:6–13, 22–23

I don't think this guy just stumbled on the street and happened to find the woman there. I bet he had heard about her reputation and had probably seen her before. But he went down the road anyway. It was dark—he was at the wrong place and he knew it.

We all know there are things we need to avoid in order to fight temptation before temptation comes. What do you need to do now to make sure you are not giving in to temptation? We can't stop every temptation, but we sure can cut down the risk of getting ambushed by knowing where the fire is that we don't want to get burned by.

We gravitate towards what we focus on. Our thoughts are filled by what we allow ourselves to think about. Quit looking at the problem, and instead focus on the answer. When we fill our minds, mouths and hearts with God's Word, the light will drive out the darkness.

THEREFORE THEN, since we are surrounded by so great a cloud of witnesses [who have borne testimony to the Truth], let us strip off and throw aside every encumbrance (unnecessary weight) and that sin which so readily (deftly and cleverly) clings to and entangles us, and let us run with patient endurance and steady and active persistence the appointed course of the race that is set before us, Looking away [from all that will distract] to Jesus, Who is the Leader and the Source of our faith [giving the first incentive for our belief] and is also its Finisher [bringing it to maturity and perfection]. He, for the joy [of obtaining the prize] that was set before Him, endured the cross, despising and ignoring the shame, and is now seated at the right hand of the throne of God.
~HEBREWS 12:1–2 AMP

Saint, you have been given freedom, power and authority to live your life to the full, just the way God intended you to live! Use God's Word; speak to your mountain!

Blow the Lid Off
Romans 12

Being part of the family of God means we need to be busy with the family business. And God's business so much more than simply attending church services; we are to be a Service Church.

In a church service you can walk in, sit down and let everybody else do the work around you, but in a Service Church, you are the one taking care of business so that others can hear about Jesus. If you want to know God's good and perfect will for your life, then get busy taking care of his people. Get into building his church. Use what you have been given to advance God's kingdom on earth so that many others can hear about Jesus and invite him into their lives.

Take care of what concerns God and he will take care of what concerns you. We often limit ourselves by limiting God. If we are going to see the good news of Jesus Christ spread in our generation, we are going to have to "blow the lid off" what is holding us back.

Here are a few steps to help you accomplish that goal:

1. Allow the Holy Spirit to "fire you up."

*Never be lacking in zeal, but keep your spiritual fervor,
serving the Lord.* ~ROMANS 12:11

It seems like the further some get away from their "day of salvation" the less "fire" they have in them. A lukewarm "I don't want to rock the boat" attitude slithers into the place the once-fiery "I can do all things" confession used to occupy.

There are a number of dynamics that can influence this "cooling off," an important one being the people we hang around with. If they aren't much for "onward and upward," chances are they are comfortable just spending their time and energy treading water—not getting washed downstream but also not moving forward.

Even more deceptive can be our own familiarity with God's Word. When we begin to feel like we know what it says and what we are supposed to do, we tend to ignore our need to keep reading it. "I've heard it all before . . . I'm doing fine"—this is a wet blanket that douses the Holy Spirit's fire. Let's look at Romans 12:1.

*Therefore, I urge you, brothers, in view of God's mercy,
to offer your bodies as living sacrifices, holy and
pleasing to God—this is your spiritual act of worship.*

We are supposed to give our bodies as a sacrifice to God. That means give everything. Give every day, every breath, every step and every thought to God. He doesn't put limitations on what we are to give, he just says give. This includes our time and our focus as well. But not only that, we have each been *given* something unique to give:

*We have different gifts, according to the grace given us.
If a man's gift is prophesying, let him use it in proportion
to his faith. If it is serving, let him serve; if it is teaching,*

let him teach; if it is encouraging, let him encourage; if it is contributing to the needs of others, let him give generously; if it is leadership, let him govern diligently; if it is showing mercy, let him do it cheerfully. ~ROMANS 12:6–8

God gave you gifts and he wants you to use them. When you use them he will give you more. Do you think you have only one gift? Then use that gift and you will be given more.

...to everyone who has, more will be given, but as for the one who has nothing, even what he has will be taken away. ~LUKE 19:26

It's like muscles in general: "Use 'em or lose 'em!"

2. Chill out.

Be joyful in hope, patient in affliction, faithful in prayer. ~ROMANS 12:12

Hebrews 11:1 explains that "faith is being sure of what we hope for," and being "joyful in hope" is just that. It's not always easy, but when we know God has our steps mapped out because Jesus won the battle for us and is now winning the battle through us, we can face each day and its happenings with a "joyful hope."

Patience is another tough one, especially when the struggle we are facing is public knowledge. It is tough enough to deal with our own expectations, but it only fuels the fire when those around us, though well-meaning, keep asking questions about the situation we are waiting on God for, and we may feel pressure to reach the answer more quickly than God's timeline calls for. God's Word says, "be patient in affliction"—when you'd like to have had the answer "yesterday."

3. Don't let evil take you down.

Do not be overcome by evil, but overcome evil with good. ~ROMANS 12:21

"Why should I volunteer my time? There are a lot of other people to do that stuff, and I can't really do that task anyway." Becoming complacent or lazy in our service is letting evil take us down.

"*I can do everything through him who gives me strength*" (Philippians 4:13), for with God nothing is ever impossible (Luke 1:37).

So let us seize and hold fast and retain without wavering the hope we cherish and confess and our acknowledgement of it, for He Who promised is reliable (sure) and faithful to His Word. ~HEBREWS 10:23 AMP

The only way the Devil has any power over us is if we let him. And we let him when we are not busy in our service to God. We let him when we get sloppy with the Word and the world around us or we think that God can't use us to serve him.

Do not be conformed to this world (this age), [fashioned after and adapted to its external, superficial customs], but be transformed (changed) by the [entire] renewal of your mind [by its new ideals and its new attitude], so that you may prove [for yourselves] what is the good and acceptable and perfect will of God, even the thing which is good and acceptable and perfect [in His sight for you]. ~ROMANS 12:2 AMP

Do not let evil take you down! The devil is betting that you are going to cave in, that you're going to conform (adjust, adapt, fit) to the world's ways of thinking and doing. God's Word says don't fall for it—renew your mind, renew your thoughts and take them captive. Daydream about God's Word and what he says you can do. Learn what God's will is for your life.

Here is God's will:

Don't conform to this world, keep your mind, (thoughts), full of the Word of God, (so full that it flows out of your mouth), that your thoughts, (meditations), become actions.

Then the devil will "run in terror" from you. Do not let evil take you down! The gifts God has put in you are for serving him by serving his church. Your gifts aren't simply for you to use for your satisfaction and pleasure, although that is a spin-off of using your gifts correctly. Your gifts are to be used to bring God glory as you use them within the local church. If you use the gifts he gives you in his service, then you will be living his perfect will.

Saint, step up and step out; don't sit back and let others do all the work. Blow the lid off the confines of what you think you can do—those thought are limiting God in your life! Put your gifts to work in the kingdom so more will be poured into your life (Luke 6:38).

Take care of what concerns God and he will take care of what concerns you. You are blessed to be a blessing, Saint!

Branch or Stick?
John 15:1-21

Six times in the first seven verses of this passage, Jesus said, "Remain in me" or "Remain in the vine," so it shouldn't be to tough to figure out what he's trying to tell us here. And yet, we make conscious choices to skip reading his Word and doing his will, neglecting to even check in with him to see what he would like us to accomplish during the day ahead of us.

Staying connected to Jesus means the difference between life or death, and of course we "know" this, but somehow we conclude that it's okay to do our agenda items first and God's agenda later, when we *think* we will have time for him. However, in his illustration of the vine and the branches, Jesus did not make concessions for those who would walk away from his plan. If we disengage, we are lost.

It only makes sense. For instance, if you get up in the morning and go to the fridge and everything is warm inside; or if you turn the switch on in the bathroom but the light doesn't come on; or if you get into you car, turn the key, but hear nothing but silence, what do you conclude? There has been a disconnection from the power source. Likewise, in order to live your life with power, you have to stay connected to the Source.

1. Branches stay connected to stay alive. (John 15:1–5)

I am the true vine, and my Father is the gardener. He cuts off every branch in me that bears no fruit, while every branch that does bear fruit he prunes so that it will be even more fruitful. You are already clean because of the word I have spoken to you. Remain in me, and I will remain in you. No branch can bear fruit by itself; it must remain in the vine. Neither can you bear fruit unless you remain in me. I am the vine; you are the branches. If a man remains in me and I in him, he will bear much fruit; apart from me you can do nothing.

The only way to be a "branch" is to follow Jesus. Those who do not have Jesus Christ as their Lord and Saviour are not connected to him. They call out to him when they're in trouble but they change their tune when the trouble passes. They think he hears them but they are not "connected"— they are not receiving the living "sap," the life blood, from the "vine." They are not branches, they are sticks. No life flows in them or through them.

Just so we don't lie to ourselves, Jesus shows us how to tell if we are really "in him." The one purpose in the vine is fruit-bearing: "fruit" (v. 1), "more fruit" (v. 2), and "much fruit" (v. 5). One who is filled with the Spirit (sap) produces the Fruit of the Spirit (Galatians 5:22–23). So, we need to ask ourselves if, or better, "prove" to ourselves that we are not simply sticks but branches, and not just branches but strong, healthy limbs connected to Jesus, the "Vine."

Are you producing fruit? Is there fruit, more fruit, and much fruit being produced in your life? Nowhere does

Jesus approve of "little" fruit—a berry here and there, a thin bunch of sour grapes. No, Jesus came to give us life to the full! We have all been given gifts to use in the building of God's Kingdom, and if we are not using what we've been given for his glory, the little that we have will be taken from us. (*Check out Matthew 25:14–30 to clarify what I am saying here.*)

Remember what happened in Matthew 21:19 when Jesus looked for fruit on a fig tree and found none?

> *Seeing a fig tree by the road, he went up to it but found nothing on it except leaves. Then he said to it, "May you never bear fruit again!" Immediately the tree withered.*

What was that all about? The tree made it look like it was producing fruit, but it wasn't. If ever a tree were a "poser" thus was it. Serious stuff! If you are connected to the Vine, you will produce fruit.

2. Disciples imitate their leader. (John 15:8–12 AMP)

> *When you bear (produce) much fruit, My Father is honored and glorified, and you show and prove yourselves to be true followers of Mine. I have loved you, [just] as the Father has loved Me; abide in My love [continue in His love with Me]. If you keep My commandments [if you continue to obey My instructions], you will abide in My love and live on in it, just as I have obeyed My Father's commandments and live on in His love. I have told you these things, that My joy and delight may be in you, and that your joy and gladness may be of full measure and complete and overflowing. This is My commandment: that you love one another [just] as I have loved you.*

When the branch is connected to the vine, it fulfills its intended purpose.

> *So Jesus said to those Jews who had believed in Him, If you abide in My word [hold fast to My teachings and live in accordance with them], you are truly My disciples.*
> ~JOHN 8:31 AMP

True discipleship involves a readiness to learn and do, to apply and believe every word.

> *If you remain in me and my words remain in you, ask whatever you wish, and it will be given you.* ~JOHN 15:7

3. Friends take time to talk. (John 15:14–15)

> *You are My friends if you keep on doing the things which I command you to do. I do not call you servants (slaves) any longer, for the servant does not know what his master is doing (working out). But I have called you My friends, because I have made known to you everything that I have heard from My Father. [I have revealed to you everything that I have learned from Him.]*

A friend can get far closer to the heart of the Master than a servant can.

Think about this. We are called Jesus' friends! We walk around and go about our daily business as if it's no big deal. Come on, think about it! If the President of the United States, the Queen of England or our Prime Minister were to give you a call and say, "Hey, what's up? Do you what to hang out today?" that would be cool. I'm fairly sure you'd be letting everyone around you know that you were going to hang out with such a significant person.

But far more wonderful is the fact that we not only get to call Jesus our friend, he says we're *his* friends and we get to hang out with him when ever we want (which, hopefully, is all the time). Friends talk. Friends share. We are friends with Jesus, so let's talk to him and take the time to listen to what he has to say to us. Because we are connected to Jesus' HEART in this way, we get to share in his secrets.

> *The secret [of the sweet, satisfying companionship] of the Lord have they who fear (revere and worship) Him, and He will show them His covenant and reveal to them its [deep, inner] meaning. ~PSALM 25:14 AMP*

As friends of God, we have the power to live with hope in a condemned world because we know the secrets to life, peace and eternal glory.

We are able to love what he loves and hate what he hates:

> *These six things the Lord hates, indeed, seven are an abomination to Him: A proud look [the spirit that makes one overestimate himself and underestimate others], a lying tongue, and hands that shed innocent blood, A heart that manufactures wicked thoughts and plans, feet that are swift in running to evil, A false witness who breathes out lies [even under oath], and he who sows discord among his brethren. ~PROVERBS 6:16–19 AMP*

> *The reverent fear and worshipful awe of the Lord [includes] the hatred of evil; pride, arrogance, the evil way, and perverted and twisted speech I hate. ~PROVERBS 8:13 AMP*

. . . and to share in his sufferings.

If you belonged to the world, the world would treat you with affection and would love you as its own. But because you are not of the world [no longer one with it], but I have chosen (selected) you out of the world, the world hates (detests) you. ~JOHN 15:19 AMP

The more we become like Jesus, the more we will feel darkness pushing against us.

Consider it pure joy, my brothers, whenever you face trials of many kinds . . . ~JAMES 1:2

To this you were called, because Christ suffered for you, leaving you an example, that you should follow in his steps. ~1 PETER 2:21

For just as the sufferings of Christ flow over into our lives, so also through Christ our comfort overflows. ~2 CORINTHIANS 1:5

What God was to Jesus, so the Holy Spirit is to us: an all-sufficient Comforter. There isn't anything you can accomplish without Jesus that's going to last. There is no true lasting happiness and satisfaction without Jesus. There is no hope apart from Jesus.

Stay connected, Saint!

Reading John's Gospel

This morning I was reading Chapter 14 of the Gospel of John and a couple points jumped out at me, so I thought, hey, why not share them with you?

Jesus answered, "I am the way and the truth and the life. No one comes to the Father except through me." ~JOHN 14:6

Jesus is the ONLY way. Most, if not all, of us would agree to that, but too many times we still try with our good works and our good deeds to somehow earn something we already have. When we do this, what we are actually saying is, "My way is better than the route Jesus Christ took on my behalf." See what I mean? That's not being humble—that's being stupid. Why strive to get something you already have?

It's all about the FINISHED work of the Cross; it's not about us tossing in our "two cents" to see if we can add something to make Jesus' sacrifice more effective. Jesus, and Jesus alone is the ONLY way to heaven, the ONLY way to peace and blessing in your life.

Believe me when I say that I am in the Father and the Father is in me; or at least believe on the evidence of the miracles themselves. I tell you the truth, anyone who has faith in me will do what I have been doing. He will do even greater things than these, because I am going to the Father. And I will do whatever you ask in my name, so that the Son may bring glory to the Father. You may ask me for anything in my name, and I will do it. ~JOHN 14:11–14

Do you believe Jesus?

Be careful now; think about your answer. Do you think you would live differently if you really believed? Jesus said we can ask him for ANYTHING in his name. He said it himself: "I WILL DO IT." Do you believe he will? It's not just asking for whatever or whenever, it is asking according to his Word.

Too many people don't really KNOW God's Word. Of course they say they do, but when it comes to boldly asking God for something (Hebrews 4:16), they just kind of resort to the generic "bless me, Lord" types of prayers. Now listen, I am not trying to condemn anyone here; I want to sound an alarm to get serious with God, to get serious about who he is and who you ARE as his chosen child (Isaiah 41:9). God tells us that people die because they don't "know."

My people are destroyed from lack of knowledge. ~HOSEA 4:6

Trusting Jesus to be the Way, the Truth and the Life takes faith (Hebrews 11:1).

Faith looks at the outrageous claims of God's Word and considers them to be so! Faith does not try to make them happen. Trying to make them happen gives testimony to the fact that you do not believe they have already happened. You can't make Jesus be crucified. He was crucified. You can't make Jesus rise from the dead. He has risen. You can't make him Lord; he is Lord! And you can't make yourself free from the

*limitations of your past existence. You are free. All of
these things are the glory of God. All we can do is
consider them so. Faith accepts God's view and opinion
as a present reality. When God's opinion becomes our
opinion, his reality will become ours then we will
experience life in Christ as it really is.*[2]

In John 14:30 Jesus says, ". . . *the prince of this world
[the devil] is coming. He has no hold on me.*" As well, in
John 14:20 Jesus says, "*I am in my Father, and you are in
me, and I am in you.*" We are in Christ (Colossians 3:3)
and the devil has NO hold on Jesus, which also means he
has NO hold on us because we are the body of Christ. We
have the Holy Spirit in us (2 Corinthians 1:22) and
therefore the devil has NO rights to us.

We need to stop thinking like victims, blaming the devil
for everything that goes wrong. If we do not really "know"
the truth, we will, more than likely, fall for a lie. The enemy
will come around and toss something your way, and if you
are not speaking out the Word and standing on it, you will
end up jumping for it because you weren't keeping your
eyes on Jesus (Hebrews 12:2).

Let me encourage you, this is easily combated by
getting into the Word, learning it, knowing it and speaking
it to every situation you come across today.

No one is here "just because." If you were not needed in
the plans God has, you most certainly wouldn't be taking
up space on this planet.

The Lord has made this day, so live it to the fullest. You
have a very special part to play in it!

---

[2] Dr. James B. Richards, *Becoming the Person You Want to Be*
(Huntsville, AL: Milestones International Publishers, 2004) p.117.

Follower
Psalm 26

Whuen we give our lives to Jesus, he not only sets us free from our sins (past, present and future), he also gives us the right to become his children (John 1:12). As his children, he tells us to love those around us the way he loves us.

If we want to serve God, then we need to serve the ones he loves, not because we have to but because we understand that whatever we do to others we are doing to Jesus (Matthew 25:40). Jesus is not asking us to do something he wouldn't.

> *. . . just as the Son of Man did not come to be served, but to serve, and to give his life as a ransom for many.*
> ~MATTHEW 20:28

Jesus gave up his life in heaven to serve us as our scapegoat, to carry our sin and our punishment even when we could have cared less about him, the cross or anything else, for that matter! (Romans 5:8).

In Psalm 26 David exhibits some great qualities as a servant of God. As you read, take some time to look at yourself and what you are doing and see how you compare.

*Vindicate me, O Lord, for I have led a blameless life; I
have trusted in the Lord without wavering. Test me, O
Lord, and try me, examine my heart and my mind; for
your love is ever before me, and I walk continually in
your truth.* ~Psalm 26:1–3

"Vindicate" means, to clear, pardon or defend. When
we serve God by serving others, we can rely on God to
defend us, and when our hearts are focused on his
commandments and plans, we can expect pardon when we
make mistakes.

"*Test me...*" In your prayer time, stop and ask, "Lord, is
there something blocking me from hearing you better?" He
will show you what has stolen the time you used to spend
with him. He won't condemn you for it; he will just point
out areas where you have drifted (Romans 8:1).

We can be easily distracted by the continual "movie" of
thoughts and memories running through our minds all day
long, and sometimes these thoughts can lead us down
paths we should not go. How is your thought life doing?
Would you like the Lord to examine your mind and your
thoughts and the heart behind those thoughts?

A good servant checks himself out (not everyone else)
to see if he is doing what he said he would. We need to
open ourselves up to God in our prayer times and allow his
Holy Spirit to give us a check-up (2 Corinthians 13:5).

Usually, when you go to a doctor for a check-up, he or
she will take a tongue depressor, hold your tongue down
and take a look inside your mouth. I think that's what we
need to allow the Holy Spirit to do to us—only he will check
what is coming *out* of our mouths, the integrity of the
words we speak.

Get off the bench.

*I do not sit with deceitful men, nor do I consort with
hypocrites; I abhor the assembly of evildoers and refuse
to sit with the wicked. I wash my hands in innocence,
and go about your altar, O Lord. ~PSALM 26:4–6*

There are times when the crowd we hang out with is
not going the way we have chosen to go in our spiritual life.
We need to walk away from those situations for a time.
This doesn't change the important fact that those who
don't know about Jesus need us to tell them, but what I am
saying is that we need to get off the bench of wrong
thinking and speaking so we can be faithful to the way we
have chosen through Christ to live.

*You adulterous people, don't you know that friendship
with the world is hatred toward God? Anyone who
chooses to be a friend of the world becomes an enemy
of God. ~JAMES 4:4*

*Do not be yoked together with unbelievers. For what do
righteousness and wickedness have in common? Or what
fellowship can light have with darkness? ~2 CORINTHIANS 6:14*

Be careful who and what you join forces with, especially
those who will stop you from doing the Lord's work.

Be Thankful.

*. . . proclaiming aloud your praise and telling of all your
wonderful deeds. I love the house where you live, O
Lord, the place where your glory dwells. ~PSALM 26:7–8*

We will shout for joy when you are victorious and will lift up our banners in the name of our God. May the Lord grant all your requests. ~PSALM 20:5 NIV

Sing to him a new song; play skillfully, and shout for joy. ~PSALM 33:3

Sharing our faith isn't as much preaching as it is just lifting up the name of the Lord, telling people what God has done in our lives and how we've seen God perform miracles in and around us.

. . . faith comes from hearing the message, and the message is heard through the word of Christ. ~ROMANS 10:17

Serving God is serving others. God looked at us all and felt we were worth the cost of the life of his Son, Jesus; he sent Jesus to take the penalty of our sin so that we could be together with him.

God sees each person as precious. His servants do too, and their lives are spent demonstrating it to the people around them.

Are you interested in going forward in God's best? Step up and step out—be a servant.

Thinking About Frogs

How do you a boil a live frog without it knowing you're tying to cook it? (Answer) You turn up the heat slowly. The frog gets used to each level of heat and adapts to its environment, not realizing that it's being cooked alive and the end is far closer than it might imagine.

I have benefited from asking myself some tough questions, and I want to share them with you:

1. Can you remember a time when you laughed more than you do now?
2. Can you recall a time when you enjoyed life more than you do now?
3. Are you praying less than you have before, spending less time in God's Word than you used to?

As you consider your answers, my point here is to help you discover if maybe you're edging, ever so slowly, away from "life"—from God. Perhaps the heat is being adjusted so subtly that you can just adapt to where your life is at, not realizing that without a conscious decision to step up your fellowship with God the distance between you will continue to lengthen. This is what it means to become "lukewarm."

> *I know your [record of] works and what you are doing;*
> *you are neither cold nor hot. Would that you were cold or*
> *hot! So, because you are lukewarm and neither cold nor*
> *hot, I will spew you out of My mouth! For you say, I am*
> *rich; I have prospered and grown wealthy, and I am in*
> *need of nothing; and you do not realize and understand*
> *that you are wretched, pitiable, poor, blind, and naked.*
> *~REVELATION 3:15–17 AMP*

God takes "lukewarmness" very seriously, so we would do well to understand how to avoid its dangers. So, what does it look like?

First of all, "lukewarmness" is a process. I don't think any believer really intentionally pursues it, but it slips into one's life so slowly and smoothly that without decisive action one could stay oblivious in that state. "Lukewarmness" can come in when you get disappointed about your dreams or how you thought life would turn out. Disappointment gives way to disillusionment, and we start to lose our focus. Then disillusionment gives way to indifference—the "whatever" or "who cares" attitude—which gives birth to cynicism.

A cynic can actually make their miserable situation sound funny. They seem to make light of it, but really they've just given up and don't care anymore, so they dress it up with jokes. It's amazing how silently "lukewarm" can overtake passion.

Look at this:

> *But I have this [one charge to make] against you: that*
> *you have left (abandoned) the love that you had at first*
> *[you have deserted Me, your first love]. ~REVELATION 2:4 AMP*

If you've slipped away from times with God, time in his Word, time in prayer, it's not too late to get back to it. You're not too far gone—no way!

> *So Jesus said to those Jews who had believed in Him, If you abide in My word [hold fast to My teachings and live in accordance with them], you are truly My disciples. And you will know the Truth, and the Truth will set you free.*
> ~JOHN 8:31–32 AMP

God's Word is truth! And when you read it and apply it, the truth is revealed to you. You can say all you want that you believe God's Word is true, but if you don't put it into action, what good is it to you?

> *For if anyone only listens to the Word without obeying it and being a doer of it, he is like a man who looks carefully at his [own] natural face in a mirror; For he thoughtfully observes himself, and then goes off and promptly forgets what he was like. But he who looks carefully into the faultless law, the [law] of liberty, and is faithful to it and perseveres in looking into it, being not a heedless listener who forgets but an active doer [who obeys], he shall be blessed in his doing (his life of obedience).* ~JAMES 1:23-25 AMP

We all need a good kick in the spiritual "butt" from time to time; in fact, that's what we're supposed to do for each other (Proverbs 27:17). So, I say this in love, trusting and knowing that God's Word will do exactly what he intended it to do (Isaiah 55:11). Stop and listen to the Holy Spirit, then ask yourself the questions at the top of the page. Jump out of the pot before you're cooked.

As a born again believer in Jesus Christ, you are blessed by the Lord, you have been CHOSEN by God!

(Ephesians 1:3–4) Your Life has PURPOSE—so now LIVE your life ON PURPOSE! (Jeremiah 29:11)

A Beginner's Guide to Fishing
Matthew 4:18–22

W hen Jesus came across his first disciples, Peter and Andrew, he said he was going to make them "fishers of men." I wonder if that didn't drum up visions in their minds of hooks in people's mouths or tossing massive nets over crowds, or if they just accepted the idea.

Regardless, they followed Jesus to find James and John. These two dropped what they were doing and followed Jesus—he called, and they answered! Today Jesus is calling each one of us to be "fishers of men." The call, the plan, is still the same as the day he walked the shores of the Sea of Galilee.

To be a fisherman there are things you need to know and tools you have to carry. A fisherman with an empty tackle box comes home empty-handed. We need to be ready and willing if we are going to follow Jesus and carry on the work he began.

For the Son of Man came to seek and to save what was lost. ~LUKE 19:10

Being faithful to Jesus isn't just about saying the right things and showing up at all the right places at the right times. Being faithful is about doing the very thing that is closest to his heart: going after the lost, setting them free and helping them accept the finished work of Jesus Christ on the cross.

1. The Equipment.

I don't mind fishing from time to time. One thing (one of many, actually) that separates me from a "real" fishermen, however, is that I don't have the equipment. I don't even own a fishing rod.

I once went out fishing off the shore of Alaska with some pretty hardcore fishermen. They had everything, even things in their tackle boxes that I had never seen. They had tools and string and all sorts of insect-looking things so they could make their own hooks! I thought you just went out and bought them—who knew that you could make a specific lure for a specific fish in a specific area?

Along with the right equipment, another thing they had that I didn't was commitment. Fishing was more than just a sport for them; it was a way of life. We, too, need to make "fishing for men" (sharing the gospel of Jesus Christ) a way of life, to be hardcore about living out the faith we claim to have. Showing up with an empty basket when the fishermen are showing off the day's catch isn't a good thing. But I can only imagine at best what it would be like entering eternity with no souls won for Jesus. When we give our lives to Jesus, one of the things we must do is share that saving Word with others. Jesus said, "I will make you fishers of men."

Now, I'm not talking about a pushy, "cram it down their throats " agenda, but rather, handling the Word of

God the way it was intended (2 Timothy 2:15). The bait has to be attractive. Fish aren't going to bite at any old boot hung from a rope!

> *You are the light of the world. A city on a hill cannot be hidden. Neither do people light a lamp and put it under a bowl. Instead they put it on its stand, and it gives light to everyone in the house. In the same way, let your light shine before men, that they may see your good deeds and praise your Father in heaven.* ~MATTHEW 5:14–16

Have you ever taken a look at the fishing section of a store? Just seeing all those lures and hooks and highly polished things just about makes me want to bite into them, especially those "gummy worm" lures. If you plan on attracting anybody to the gospel, you have to be able to talk to them, and you can't do that if they don't allow you to approach them because you look like just another "Bible Thumper" looking for someone to pounce on.

2. Different bait for different fish.

A good fisherman has different lures in his tackle box for different fish because what attracts one type of fish may scare away another. The same is true in how you attract and approach different people. There is more than one way to tell a person about Jesus and numerous methods for drawing them close enough to examine the lure. With one you may "cut to the chase" and lay down the truth; with others you may have to wait until they have vented their anger and mistrust of Jesus. Some may take days or weeks or months to observe you to see if you can be trusted. A good fisherman knows when and how to use choose the right lure for the right fish.

3. Get the hook in the water.

(John 4:4–14, 39 gives the example of Jesus talking with the Samaritan woman at the well.)

You can't fish in your living room, and sitting in your back yard flicking the hook halfway across the lawn and then reeling it back again doesn't bring in a catch. You may be performing all the actions of fishing but there is nothing there to be caught. We have to be where people are, looking for opportunities to be "a friend of sinners," a friend to the hurting, etc. Just sitting in meeting after meeting talking about the lost and how they need Jesus isn't going to connect people with the saving Word, and hanging out with born again people all the time and not including the "pre-saved" is a sure way to avoid leading anyone to the throne of God.

Instead, we need to get out and start sharing the hope we have in Jesus Christ with those we meet at work, in the store or while out for a walk (Matthew 28:19). Fishermen know where in the lake to head for and where to cast the lure for the best chance at catching fish. They know the lake, they know their equipment, and they know where to cast because they know what attracts the fish. The same rings true for us in our pursuit of spreading the Good Word about Jesus Christ.

A fisherman isn't guaranteed to catch fish just because he goes out, but he goes out all the same. If he doesn't catch a fish with the first cast, he reels the line back in and casts again. If he doesn't catch any fish that day, he goes out again the next. Many fishermen go out and catch nothing, but none of those guys quit, saying, "I guess it's just not my calling." Fishermen keep going out day after day, year after year, because they want to catch fish!

You need to understand that you can't save anyone; it's all about what God has done and not about what you have done. God calls, you fish! It's not up to you who comes to Jesus (John 3:8; 6:44), but it is your job to go throw out the net. Fishing for people is all about your faithfulness and obedience to God and his Word.

Clean out that tackle box, sharpen up the hooks, polish the lures—you have a calling on your life! It's not about how many people you lead to the Lord, it's about how faithful you are in handling the Word of Truth.

How willing you are to allow Jesus to work in and through you to make you the highly polished lure that will attract people to you so you can tell them about Jesus?

I'm putting up my sign right now: Gone Fishin'!

Bring It In

When a farmer purchases a new piece of equipment, like a combine, for instance, he has to lay down some serious cash. New combines will run you about $280,000! That's a whole lot of money!

After he gets it home, he doesn't just sit beside it in the machine shop. If it's harvest time, that combine is out in the fields doing what the farmer purchased it for: bringing in the harvest. Sure, he does his part to look after it, keeping it filled with oil and fuel, but he still expects it to do the work it was designed for.

In Luke chapter 15 we find three different parables: one about a lost sheep, the next about a lost coin and lastly, the lost son. All three are stories about finding or reclaiming what was lost. Jesus wants us to know he is concerned about the lost, those who do not know him.

In Mark 12:28 a teacher of the Law asked Jesus which was the most important commandment:

"The most important one," answered Jesus, "is this: 'Hear, O Israel, the Lord our God, the Lord is one. Love the Lord your God with all your heart and with all your soul and with all your mind and with all your strength.' The second

is this: 'Love your neighbor as yourself.' There is no commandment greater than these." ~MARK 12:29–31

Love God and love people. Loving people means that you do what someone did for you—that is, you tell them about Jesus.

When we give our lives to Jesus, it's like the farmer and the combine. Jesus doesn't want us to just sit around and look good. He wants us looking good out in the field bringing in the harvest.
Jesus laid down his life in obedience to God the Father to make a way out of sin and the punishment of hell. Now he is asking us to lay down our lives for the lost.

My command is this: Love each other as I have loved you. Greater love has no one than this, that he lay down his life for his friends. ~JOHN 15:12–13

It's like Jesus is looking past us to see what we can and should be doing to reach the lost.

Suppose one of you has a hundred sheep and loses one of them. Does he not leave the ninety-nine in the open country and go after the lost sheep until he finds it? And when he finds it, he joyfully puts it on his shoulders and goes home. Then he calls his friends and neighbors together and says, "Rejoice with me; I have found my lost sheep." I tell you that in the same way there will be more rejoicing in heaven over one sinner who repents than over ninety-nine righteous persons who do not need to repent. ~LUKE 15:4–7

Jesus didn't die a painful disgusting death on the cross just so we can sit pretty and not get our hands dirty. Not a chance! The harvest is ready.

The harvest is plentiful, but the workers are few. Ask the Lord of the harvest, therefore, to send out workers into his harvest field. Go! I am sending you out like lambs among wolves. ~LUKE 10:2–3

- *What worth does a combine have to a farmer if it just sits in the shop?*

- *What good is a combine that takes up space but never does what it was designed for?*

- *Why would a farmer even want a combine that looks the part but doesn't work?*

We need to be concerned with what Jesus is concerned with. When we look after what concerns God, God will look after what concerns us (Matthew 6:33).

In late fall in the community I grew up in, you could see where the harvest was taking place for miles around because of the dust clouds that the combines would make as they brought in the harvest. Looking out towards the fields, there could be no doubt in anyone's mind that the job was getting done.

Are you kicking up any dust? It's time to bring it in—the harvest is ready.

We are therefore Christ's ambassadors, as though God were making his appeal through us. We implore you on Christ's behalf: Be reconciled to God. ~2 CORINTHIANS 5:20

A Look @ ME
Luke 6:43–49

It's good for us to reflect and evaluate what we are doing for the Lord and how we are handling his Word. In doing this, however, we need to be careful that we don't lean too far to one side or the other. We can get to the point of feeling we're completely useless for the work of the Lord or we can swing over to the other side and feel everything we do is perfect and life is peachy. As the saying goes: For every mile of road there are two miles of ditch.

What am I growing in my life? (Luke 6:43–46)

No good tree bears bad fruit, nor does a bad tree bear good fruit. Each tree is recognized by its own fruit. People do not pick figs from thorn-bushes, or grapes from briers. The good man brings good things out of the good stored up in his heart, and the evil man brings evil things out of the evil stored up in his heart. For out of the overflow of his heart his mouth speaks.

Good fruit. Are we supposed to have figs or grapes growing out of our ears or sprouting from the backs of our heads? No, that's not the type of fruit being referred to here. Look at Galatians 5:22–26.

But the fruit of the Spirit is love, joy, peace, patience, kindness, goodness, faithfulness, gentleness and self-control. Against such things there is no law. Those who belong to Christ Jesus have crucified the sinful nature with its passions and desires. Since we live by the Spirit, let us keep in step with the Spirit. Let us not become conceited, provoking and envying each other.

Oftentimes we compare ourselves to each other, particularly those we know aren't doing well, so we can feel good about ourselves because their struggles make us look good. However, we aren't supposed to compare ourselves to others; we are supposed to hold up the Word of God and measure ourselves to what the Word says we are suppose to be. When we do that we get the real picture of who we are and how we are doing.

For instance, the second fruit of the Spirit is joy. Joy doesn't mean you are always bouncing off the walls; joy shows itself in confident peace even though you are in the middle of a storm. How are you doing with joy in your life? What about peace, patience, kindness, goodness, faithfulness, gentleness and self-control?

Note that these are all fruits "of the Spirit." You can't fake them or buy them; they come as a gift from God through the Holy Spirit. These nine fruits of the Spirit are the ruler we are to measure ourselves against, not other people. Just saying you are living for the Lord will not benefit anyone, including yourself, but when you accept and apply the fruits of the Spirit in your life, those fruits will prove the position you truly hold. If you really want to grow in your walk with the Lord, pay attention to these nine areas of your life.

Who's first? (Luke 6:46)

Why do you call me, "Lord, Lord," and do not do what I say?

You see, we are talking about self-evaluation. This isn't about looking at the people you live with or work with or about blaming a program for your inability to move forward. Verse 46 is clear: "Why do you call me, 'Lord, Lord,' and do not do what I say?"

Who we place in the seat of importance in our lives is made clear by the fruit we are producing or the lack thereof. When Jesus is Lord of your life, you will do what Jesus says to do. That takes the focus off of "me" and "mine" and puts it on the needs of others.

> *. . . just as the Son of Man did not come to be served, but to serve, and to give his life as a ransom for many.*
> *~MATTHEW 20:28*

Jesus had full rights to demand service as the very Son of God, but he didn't. He took the position of a servant, giving his life for those who mocked him.

What are you standing on? (Luke 6:47–48)

> *I will show you what he is like who comes to me and hears my words and puts them into practice. He is like a man building a house, who dug down deep and laid the foundation on rock. When a flood came, the torrent struck that house but could not shake it, because it was well built.*

A person who hears and obeys Jesus has built their house on the rock. Their house will stand and they will not be rattled when storms come. A person who hears and disobeys Jesus has built their house on the sand. That house won't make it; there is no foundation—they heard a lot of the Word but never really applied it. When tough times come they crumble because they have nothing solid to stand on.

Storms do not strengthen us; storms come to tear down, push over and wreck. Rather, storms show the strength of what the house is built on. If we are not completely convinced that God will never leave us and that his plans for us are perfect, I can tell you right now that we won't be able to stand through the storms of life—and it's not *if* the storms come, it's *when* the storms come. James says that when we doubt we become like a wave of the sea getting knocked one way then another. He also says that people like that should not expect to get anything from God! (James 1:6–7).

Self-evaluation isn't about beating yourself up; it's about going to God's Word (not to everyone around you) and checking your level of obedience to his Word (Psalm 119:105; Hebrews 4:12).

Often we are afraid to run to God when we come face to face with our weaknesses and failings. It's as though we feel God recognizes our faults the same way we see them in ourselves. However, nothing could be further from the truth. God loves us in spite of our struggles and mistakes. It's not as though he is shocked or taken by surprise when we sin. He is well aware that we cannot live this life on our own strength and we need to depend on him to accept and welcome us even when we are marred by the stain of sin.

> *Let us then approach the throne of grace with confidence, so that we may receive mercy and find grace to help us in our time of need.* ~HEBREWS 4:16

Calm in the Storm

I've been out on the ocean in a 12-person Zodiac, dipping through waves. One second you're up at the top of a wave, able to see for miles, the next second you're down in a trough with massive walls of water surrounding you, blocking out any chance of seeing anything else.

But what I am describing wasn't a storm; it was a great day out on the ocean. We were out chasing whales. The whole expedition was planned out. The captain had no worries. We were told to hang on to a cord that wrapped around the boat and not to let go at any time for any reason. Once we got on those roller coaster waves I soon figured out why letting go of the cord would be a poor choice.

In Mark 4:35–41, the disciples found themselves in a boat with Jesus. He was in the back having a nap when a powerful storm whipped up. It's hard to imagine what that storm was like, but it must have been massive, because these guys were fishermen who had spent their lifetime on the water and there was something about this storm that scared (terrified) them badly.

They moved quickly to the back of the boat to wake up Jesus, who was in a deep sleep, asking him, "Don't you care if we drown?" In my imagination I see them speaking loud and fast in a really panicked tone, spit flying as the wind whips the words right out of their mouths!

Verses 39 and 40 tell us what happened next:

He got up, rebuked the wind and said to the waves, "Quiet! Be still!" Then the wind died down and it was completely calm. He said to his disciples, "Why are you so afraid? Do you still have no faith?"

You don't have to go to the ocean to experience storms; they happen on dry land too. They can also take place in our heads or our hearts or our lives in general.

Unlike the disciples, however, when storms hit we don't always go running to Jesus. We either internalize the storm or relocate the storm to other places. Also unlike the disciples, we don't have to "wake" Jesus—he is fully aware of what is going on.

Today you may be facing a storm. The past year may have been a stormy one for you in relationships at work or within your family. Some storms seem to last a long time but they don't stay forever. Storms come to *pass*—they are not a permanent feature. The disciples' storm ended when they called on Jesus; the same can be true for you and me today.

The disciples didn't sit around and debate between themselves what they should do; they brought their problem to Jesus. They didn't analyze the storm and ask each others' opinions of it; they took their trouble to the top.

Teacher, don't you care if we drown? ~v. 38

Too often when storms rage through our lives, we spend our time telling everybody else about how hard it is when we should be calling out to Jesus.

> *He got up, rebuked the wind and said to the waves, "Quiet! Be still!" Then the wind died down and it was completely calm. ~v. 39*

Did you catch that? They called on Jesus. He told the sea to be quiet and the storm was gone.

- *Where they still in a boat? Yes!*

- *Where they still out at sea? Yes!*

- *Where they safe? Yes!*

When storms rage, call out to Jesus. Look to him. A massive storm one minute can be calm and peace the next. Jesus didn't leave his friends out in a boat by themselves to battle the storm. No, he was right there with them, and the same is true for you and me today! Storms are going to come but Jesus is with us. He has given us his Holy Spirit.

Fear, panic, worry and doubt all are part of the enemy's plans to shipwreck you. They are not a part of God's master plan to strengthen you. When we go through the battles of life standing on God's Word, we come out stronger. Storms serve to test the strength of our foundation.

> *Every good gift and every perfect (free, large, full) gift is from above; it comes down from the Father of all [that gives] light, in [the shining of] Whom there can be no variation [rising or setting] or shadow cast by His turning [as in an eclipse]. ~JAMES 1:17 AMP*

Fear not [there is nothing to fear], for I am with you; do not look around you in terror and be dismayed, for I am your God. I will strengthen and harden you to difficulties, yes, I will help you; yes, I will hold you up and retain you with My [victorious] right hand of rightness and justice.
~ISAIAH 41:10 AMP

Storms are going to come, and to make it through in good condition to the other side you need to know how to navigate your life in times when it appears all is going to be lost. When others are running on panic and "what if's," you can steer through to the calm. This is accomplished by knowing God and his Word, by knowing what his Word says about who you are as a child of the Most High God and what Jesus has accomplished for you by his death and resurrection.

My people are destroyed from lack of knowledge. ~HOSEA 4:6A

When you know who you are, whose you are and the authority that has been given to you by God; when you realize that his Holy Spirit lives inside of you and understand the power available to you through the promises of God, you will see storms differently. Not only that, but you will handle them differently and come through them into calm waters.

If you don't know the authority you carry, you can't stand on it. Get into the Word, spending time praying the Word and speaking the Word over your situations. We are not to take part in panic, fear or doubt—these are not part of who we are.

For further reading, you might like to check out the blessings in Deuteronomy 28:1–13.

May the God of hope fill you with all joy and peace as you trust in him, so that you may overflow with hope by the power of the Holy Spirit. ~ROMANS 15:13

Friends

A while ago I was out walking down a street I have walked down for years. Seemingly out of nowhere, I saw a massive evergreen tree planted in someone's front yard. I walked past that yard possibly hundreds of times and never saw a tree there. When I mentioned it to a passerby, I was told that the tree had been in that same spot for some fifty or more years. I found it hard to believe. I wanted to argue my case but realized I had become so used to walking past that massive evergreen that I didn't see it.

Many of us treat our friends like I did that tree. We are around them so much that we don't see them anymore. And when they do appear we are surprised that they are there.

God has given each one gifts. He has given us abilities to use to bring glory to him. One of the ways we do that is by treating the ones he loves with the love he has for them.

Friends are such an amazing treasure. None of us do well without them. Friends are like a mirror for us. We all have blind spots, areas of our life we aren't aware of. Friends help us to see those areas. Friends also reflect the type of person we are. We need friends to sharpen us even as we sharpen them.

As iron sharpens iron, so one man sharpens another.
~PROVERBS 27:17

There are times when we have to say the hard things to a friend and equally there are times when friends have to say the hard things to us. Sometimes what they say can even sting a little, but friends can be trusted.

Wounds from a friend can be trusted, but an enemy multiplies kisses. ~PROVERBS 27:6

You don't allow just anybody you meet on the street to be your friend and speak into your life, and your friend is not the person at work that you see in the lunch room once a week. Friends have a history with you; they have a proven track record. Are friends perfect? No. You're a friend, right? Are you perfect?

A friendship doesn't just build itself; it requires a commitment. It takes being vulnerable and open to correction. Spending time with friends is not losing time; it's making time. The time we spend investing in others is time spent growing ourselves as well.

When we aim our concern and attention at others it's no longer on ourselves. When that takes place we become good soil for God to continue his perfect work in us. We become someone God can work through to bless those we come into contact with. Just like a water pipe gets wet when it carries water to a designated location, so we are blessed by being a blessing to others.

A generous man will prosper; he who refreshes others will himself be refreshed. ~PROVERBS 11:25

When we give of ourselves is when we are the most like who God intends us to be, like Jesus, and when you live your life in obedience to God's Word, he calls you friend. (John 15:14)

> *Greater love has no one than this, that he lay down his life for his friends.* ~JOHN 15:13

God loves you so much that he gave—and not just the leftovers, he gave until it hurt. God's friendship with us cost him the very life of his Son, Jesus (John 3:16; Romans 5:8).

Friendships are fantastic. I love spending time with friends. God feels the same way. He wants to spend time with us. We can do that by studying the Bible, by talking to him in prayer, by worshiping him and serving him by serving others.

Spending time with God is tremendous because great friendships come from a great relationship with Jesus. Without him at the core, everything we do is deemed useless. But with Jesus as our centre, every friendship we come into prospers (Psalm 1:3).

> *I am the vine; you are the branches. Whoever lives in Me and I in him bears much (abundant) fruit. However, apart from Me [cut off from vital union with Me] you can do nothing.* ~JOHN 15:5 AMP

Do you want great friendships? Start spending time with Jesus. Friendship is God's idea.

Be a great friend and you will attract great friends.

I am a friend of God!

God's Will

G od's will is something we all want in our lives, and yet
many of us who call Jesus our Lord seem to wrestle
with the idea of knowing God's will. In my life there
have been times when a tough decision needed to be made
and there was absolutely no doubt what God's will for that
situation was. There have also been times when his will
was somewhat elusive. I understand now that God wasn't
hiding from me—it was me not paying attention to what
was right under my nose.

As time has passed and I've walked some pretty deep,
dark paths, there are lessons that have been learned on the
way. God's Word holds many promises that say "Yes" God
wants us to know his will and "No" it's not some sort of
mysterious thing that only a select few can know.

Look at these verses:

- *We have been created in the image of God. (Genesis
  1:27)*

- *We have been given the mind of Christ. (1
  Corinthians 2:16)*

- *God has placed his Holy Spirit in us to lead us. (John
  14:26)*

- *God's promises to us are "Yes" and "Amen." (2 Corinthians 1:20)*

Do you think it is God's will that we know his will?

In John 13 we see Jesus getting up from eating with his friends to take on the role of a servant. He gets ready as the disciples sit there watching, then he, Jesus the Son of God, proceeds to wash their feet.

Let's pick up the story from verses 12–17:

When he had finished washing their feet, he put on his clothes and returned to his place. "Do you understand what I have done for you?" he asked them. "You call me 'Teacher' and 'Lord,' and rightly so, for that is what I am."

This is what I want you to see:

Now that I, your Lord and Teacher, have washed your feet, you also should wash one another's feet. I have set you an example that you should do as I have done for you. I tell you the truth, no servant is greater than his master, nor is a messenger greater than the one who sent him. Now that you know these things, you will be blessed if you do them.

Serving others is serving Christ. The Apostle Paul said,

I became a servant of this gospel by the gift of God's grace given me through the working of his power.
~EPHESIANS 3:7

We are most like Jesus when we're serving others rather than focusing on ourselves. When we act like Jesus we are in his will. You don't have to be doing large stadium crusades or ministering to gangs out on the streets. These are great things and there are people called to do them, but the will of God holds many more possibilities for each person. Do not think that the little things in life don't really get recognized by God or that if we want to make it big in the kingdom of God we have to head up some massive world-wide ministry. That really couldn't be farther from the truth. Look at what Jesus said to the disciples:

> *And if anyone gives even a cup of cold water to one of these little ones because he is my disciple, I tell you the truth, he will certainly not lose his reward.* ~MATTHEW 10:42

A cup of water? Yes something as simple as a cup of cold water given in Jesus' name gets into the record books of heaven.

Jesus also said,

> *Whoever can be trusted with very little can also be trusted with much, and whoever is dishonest with very little will also be dishonest with much.* ~LUKE 16:10

Do you want to be involved with ministering to the nations of the earth? Do you want to see hundreds, thousands, even tens of thousands come to the Lord? Then get going with what's in your hand right now. Be faithful where you're at with what you have.

Here are some simple directions from the Apostle Paul to the church in Thessalonica:

> *Now we ask you, brothers, to respect those who work hard among you, who are over you in the Lord and who admonish you. Hold them in the highest regard in love because of their work. Live in peace with each other.*
> ~1 THESSALONIANS 5:12–13

Keep your pastor daily in your prayers. Pray for those who are leading large television ministries and pray for those who are teaching you.

If it is possible, as far as it depends on you, live at peace with everyone. ~ROMANS 12:18

And we urge you, brothers, warn those who are idle, encourage the timid, help the weak, be patient with everyone. Make sure that nobody pays back wrong for wrong, but always try to be kind to each other and to everyone else. Be joyful always; pray continually; give thanks in all circumstances . . . ~1 THESSALONIANS 5:14–18A

Here is why we are instructed to do these things:

. . . for this is God's will for you in Christ Jesus. Do not put out the Spirit's fire; do not treat prophecies with contempt. Test everything. Hold on to the good. Avoid every kind of evil. ~1 THESSALONIANS 5:18–22

It doesn't really matter where you are serving God as long as you are serving him. As the saying goes: Bloom where you are planted. Just start being like Jesus right where you are at.

There are people who are watching you, people who look up to you and are waiting for you to set an example for them. God's will is for you is to be like Jesus, and that is something you can do right in your workplace, when you're out having dinner at a restaurant, in your own home or as you fill your car with gasoline. Just act like Jesus; that's his will for you. It's not about doing great things the way you define them. It's doing things that God defines as great.

Your steps are guided by God. He has plans to prosper you, to give you hope and a future. You have been made righteous by Jesus Christ. Do you think that God gave you these things just to leave you in the lurch not knowing what he has for you?

My sheep listen to my voice; I know them, and they follow me. ~JOHN 10:27

Be joyful always; pray continually; give thanks in all circumstances, for this is God's will for you in Christ Jesus. ~1 THESSALONIANS 5:16–18

When we act like Jesus we are in God's perfect will. This can be done anytime and anyplace. God's will isn't a closed system.

It's not rules, it's relationship. It's an attitude of life (1 Corinthians 1:9). The key is to focus on knowing God himself rather than merely hunting for his guidance. The better you know God, the less confusion you're going to have about what his will is.

May God himself, the God of peace, sanctify you through and through. May your whole spirit, soul and body be kept blameless at the coming of our Lord Jesus Christ. The one who calls you is faithful and he will do it. ~1 THESSALONIANS 5:23–24

Grave Clothes

If you have ever been to visit somebody in the hospital you have probably noticed that the sick are all wearing a certain type of clothing. It simply doesn't work to wear a pressed shirt and tie or a dress in the hospital when you're staying there for treatment. The clothes sick people wear in the hospital are appropriate to that environment.

If you have any business sense at all, you know that wearing a pair of ratty jeans to an interview for a CEO position wouldn't be the right thing to do. But if you were applying for city park maintenance or construction, denim would be more acceptable.

Have you heard the saying "Dress for success"? It refers to dressing up to the level you are targeting. Situations determine the dress code. Wearing the wrong clothes in the wrong place makes for misdirected communication, like wearing a track suit to a board of directors meeting—you are making a statement with what you have on.

In John chapter 11 we find the account of Lazarus. (*I suggest reading the whole story there before we continue.*) Four days after Lazarus died, Jesus showed up on the scene. Then Jesus called Lazarus out of the tomb, calling him from death to life, and the people were astonished as the previously dead man came walking out of the tomb.

> *And out walked the man who had been dead, his hands
> and feet wrapped in burial cloths (linen strips), and with
> a [burial] napkin bound around his face. Jesus said to
> them, "Free him of the burial wrappings and let him go."*
> ~JOHN 11:44 AMP

Lazarus was alive! Life came back into his body and he was once again walking and breathing, but he was still wrapped up in the grave clothes. He needed somebody to untie him and get those death rags off his living body.

There are Christians around us today, born again believers who have been called from death to life, who are still wearing their grave clothes. Living in yesterday, living in what happened to them, living in what they think "could have been if only," they are wrapped up in things that are long gone and are bound by hurts that should have been let go shortly after the events occurred. Like driving a car using only the rear-view mirror as a navigational tool, they focus on what was and is now impossible to change.

Maybe that's you. Are you living with hurts and disappointments from the past, allowing them to taint your outlook on life and God's Word? Perhaps disillusionment has slipped in because life hasn't turned out the way you thought it could or should and your dreams are slow in coming, always taunting you just beyond your reach.

Are you wearing that stuff? Those are rags of death. A lawyer wearing a hospital gown in the courtroom is as out of place as a born again believer who has been brought from death to life but is still bound with the grave clothes; the apparel no longer fits the situation.

> *Let us fix our eyes on Jesus, the author and perfecter of
> our faith . . .* ~HEBREWS 12:2A

Mary and Martha, the sisters of Lazarus, looked to Jesus when what they saw with their physical eyes was impossible. We, too, need to look with eyes of faith to determine what course of action needs to be taken (2 Corinthians 4:18).

- *Jesus came to give us life and not just life but life to the full! (John 10:10b)*

- *We have been given the mind of Christ. (1 Corinthians 2:16)*

- *We have fullness in Christ. (Colossians 2:9–10)*

But you, dear friends, build yourselves up in your most holy faith and pray in the Holy Spirit. Keep yourselves in God's love as you wait for the mercy of our Lord Jesus Christ to bring you to eternal life. Be merciful to those who doubt; snatch others from the fire and save them; to others show mercy, mixed with fear—hating even the clothing stained by corrupted flesh. ~JUDE 1:20-23

If you know someone who is tied up in grave clothes, bring in the truth, bring in God's Word. Speak it to them; pray the Word over them. Have that person confess God's powerful Word with their mouth. The enemy comes to steal and kill and destroy (John 10:10a), but when we apply God's powerful Word—speaking it and standing on it—the enemy is crushed, his deceptive power is broken and the hurts and disappointments of the past become tools for benefit instead of destruction (Romans 8:28, 37; Ephesians 6:15). Get in there and help them untie those grave clothes.

If you are feeling tied up, get into the Word of God. Get back into confessing God's promises for you. Get back into memorizing the Word. Get back and refresh the Word you've already hidden in your heart (Psalm 119:11).

> *No, in all these things we are more than conquerors through him who loved us.* ~ROMANS 8:37

> *But blessed is the man who trusts in the Lord, whose confidence is in him. He will be like a tree planted by the water that sends out its roots by the stream. It does not fear when heat comes; its leaves are always green. It has no worries in a year of drought and never fails to bear fruit.* ~JEREMIAH 17:7–8

> *Let your light so shine before men that they may see your moral excellence and your praiseworthy, noble, and good deeds and recognize and honor and praise and glorify your Father Who is in heaven.* ~MATTHEW 5:16 AMP

Be encouraged—and be an encourager! It's not appropriate for born again, blood-bought children of God to be wearing grave clothes. Take them off and get into your new wardrobe!

Justified

Worthless. ~~Useless. Hopeless.~~ You need to scratch these words from your vocabulary so you can't be labelled by them anymore.

When you feel like you have "dropped the ball," the enemy likes to creep in and, like a vandal with a can of spray paint, plaster your identity with junk that isn't true and really has nothing to do with you. The enemy knows that if he can get you to believe these lies, he has an open door to walk in and stir up every kind of disruption in your life.

Sometimes we drift from God's Word, either by not spending time reading it or by neglecting to follow its instruction. Then in times of prayer we feel weak, as if we don't matter anyway. In those moments we can feel forgotten by God, rejected and out on our own. But who is behind those thoughts and feelings?

Hmm . . . I think I smell fresh paint.

Come on, Saint, give your head a shake! How on earth can that separate you from God's love? If your communication with God is not where it could be, there is no doubt you're going to feel distant and out on your own. But stop and take a good look at who moved—God isn't moving away from you, you are moving away from him. It wasn't God, it was you!

For I am convinced that neither death nor life, neither angels nor demons, neither the present nor the future, nor any powers, neither height nor depth, nor anything else in all creation, will be able to separate us from the love of God that is in Christ Jesus our Lord. ~ROMANS 8:38–39

If you stepped off the path, get back on it. God wants to be in touch with you. He loved you so much that he sent Jesus, his only Son, to pay the price for your sin (1Corinthians 15:3; 2 Corinthians 5:21; Hebrews 9:15; 1Peter 3:18). You have to understand and believe that Jesus' death on the cross and his resurrection paid for your sin. Jesus made your justification a reality.

Therefore, since we are now justified (acquitted, made righteous, and brought into right relationship with God) by Christ's blood, how much more [certain is it that] we shall be saved by Him from the indignation and wrath of God. ~ROMANS 5:9 AMP

Let's break it down into smaller sections so we can see all that is being said here.

"Since we are now justified . . ."

Poor choices do not automatically disqualify you from heaven. When we allow our shortfalls to dictate who we are, we end up walking away from the very One who says, "You are righteous in my sight" (2 Corinthians 5:21). We are justified! If we stumble, it is not all over; there is a chance for a comeback. It's like we think it depends on us, that if we read our Bible and pray every day God is going to love us more. This is just not so. God loves us and he proved it in and through Jesus Christ.

But God shows and clearly proves His [own] love for us by the fact that while we were still sinners, Christ (the Messiah, the Anointed One) died for us. ~ROMANS 5:8 AMP

We are justified by a powerful force. The precious blood of Jesus Christ not only covered our sins but washed them away (Psalm 103:11–12).

". . . by his blood . . ."

God cannot lie. He said, "The wages of sin is death" (Romans 6:23a). You sin, you die. But Jesus came and took the hit for you. Jesus' death on the cross was the only sacrifice that satisfied God for the payment of sin.

For Christ died for sins once for all, the righteous for the unrighteous, to bring you to God. He was put to death in the body but made alive by the Spirit. ~1 PETER 3:18

There is no other way to be saved. Jesus isn't "one" of the ways to eternal life; he is the only way (John 14:6; Acts 4:12).

". . . we . . ."

It's for everybody and anybody who wants freedom from the punishment of sin. It's an all-inclusive package for those who accept Jesus into their hearts.

". . . shall be saved . . ."

We are saved! It's not a matter of "might" or "maybe" or "there is a strong likelihood"—the payment for our sin is eternally settled.

". . . through Him . . ."

Our sins—past, present and future—are replaced by righteousness because of what Jesus has done for us on the cross. Jesus is the new lens through which we can now see ourselves for who we really are.

> *Brothers, I do not consider myself yet to have taken hold of it. But one thing I do: Forgetting what is behind and straining toward what is ahead . . .* ~PHILIPPIANS 3:13

If you've made some poor choices and know you've messed up, get back up and get going; God sees you as righteous. He paid the highest ransom that will ever be paid for a human. You are justified, Saint, now live it!

> *For though a righteous man falls seven times, he rises again, but the wicked are brought down by calamity.*
> ~PROVERBS 24:16

See yourself the way God sees you. Walk in the authority God has given you. Talk to yourself, speaking God's Word over yourself, your family and every situation that comes your way. God sees your problems as opportunities to show his power and provision. You already have everything you need for a life of godliness (2 Peter 1:3).

You are justified—don't ever allow anybody to tell you differently!

Knowing God

My son, if you accept my words and store up my commands within you, turning your ear to wisdom and applying your heart to understanding, and if you call out for insight and cry aloud for understanding, and if you look for it as for silver and search for it as for hidden treasure, then you will understand the fear of the Lord and find the knowledge of God. ~PROVERBS 2:1–5

Turn your TV to most any channel and you'll probably come across something fearful. Go out to the movies and you will find that many of them are based on fear. The fear the media instils is unhealthy, and it continues to grow in your heart and mind as you think about what you saw. "What if that would happen to me when I'm walking home tonight?" This type of fear can keep a person from eating, sleeping and even enjoying life. This is unhealthy fear.

Fear can be a powerful motivator. It is able to get us to do things that without fear we'd probably never do. If there were no late fees or personal penalties, no one would pay off their credit cards or the monthly lease or mortgage on their home or car. Likewise, without a consequence, we would stop obeying traffic lights, one-way signs and speed limits. The thought of losing a driving privilege or the risk of a poor credit rating keeps us desiring and willing to stay current. That's a type of fear that motivates us to obey.

Fear can be a good thing. We generally don't drink gasoline, eat raw chicken or lean on the element of the stove with our bare hands when it's red hot. The fear is that we'll be hurt, or even worse, that we'll die if we take part in these things. Fear in this sense is beneficial because it keeps us from doing something destructive.

The Bible talks about the fear of the Lord. If we want to know God, we have to appreciate what it means to fear the Lord. We should want to understand the fear of the Lord and grow in our knowledge of God. To get to that point we are given at least four key instructions:

1. Fill up on God's Word. (v. 1)

My son, if you accept my words and store up my commands within you . . .

God's promises are conditional upon accepting his words and storing up his commands. The first point is to accept and fill up on God's Word. If you don't know his Word, how can you accept it? If you are not filling up on God's Word, how can you do as he commands? Accepting God's Word means believing it is the holy, inspired, infallible Word of God and being willing to live it out. The Bible can't be partly right and partly wrong. Accepting God's Word is doing what it says, memorizing it, applying it and speaking it so that Holy Spirit can remind you of things you have read and heard in the Word (John 14:26).

I have hidden your word in my heart that I might not sin against you. ~PSALM 119:11

2. Listen. (v. 2a)

. . . turning your ear to wisdom . . .

To know the right course of action but opt out of choosing it is actually the opposite of wisdom. If you have listened to the point of understanding, you will naturally respond with appropriate follow-through and application. For example, if your hairdo requires gel, it won't work for you just by sitting in the bottle. You can't get up in the morning, stand next to the sink where the bottle of gel is and just "get" the 'do. You have to open the bottle and apply it to your hair if you want to see results.

Listening to God's Word shows itself in action; it's cause and effect. If you say you listen to the Word but don't apply it to your life, you are not in the game. You might make it as a bench warmer, but that's it. Tune your ears to wisdom.

3. Do it. (vv. 2b–3)

. . . applying your heart to understanding, and if you call out for insight and cry aloud for understanding . . .

God wants us to know his Word. He has given us the Holy Spirit to lead us into truth (John 14:26). When you know the Word and know God's character, then you can call out for insight. The Holy Spirit is able to show us what we can't see about any situation we find ourselves in. He will highlight what you need to learn when you are reading God's Word so you can call in the promises he has given.

The more time you spend in God's Word, the clearer you understand how to apply it to your life, and the more of the Word you know, the more accurately you can call out for understanding. Call out to God—and not just in your thoughts. Ask out loud for understanding.

4. Look for it. (v. 4)

. . . and if you look for it as for silver and search for it as for hidden treasure, then you will understand the fear of the Lord and find the knowledge of God.

If someone told you the location of a massive stash of loot that would be yours if you went for it, there's a good chance there would be little that would stop you from searching it out. When we want something in our physical lives like new clothing or a house or a car, we apply ourselves and go after it, allowing nothing to stop us from the goals we set. It is to be the same with the Word of God; the Bible tells us to go after it like we are looking for hidden treasure.

If you want to live in the miraculous, you need to know the Miracle Maker. If you want to operate in the power of God, then get to know him. This isn't done by skipping over his Word once a week—fill up on God's Word, listen to God's Word, learn God's Word and go after his Word in an unstoppable way.

Meeting "Her"—Wisdom

It has happened millions of times. A guy finds the woman of his dreams, goes after her, captures her heart and becomes one flesh with her in marriage. In the courting stage the male will go to great lengths to woo the female. Money, time and energy are all resources that the man is willing to pour out in abundance for his bride. Men have worked all day and driven for hours to spend just a short while with their love. Then they drive hours home only to find that the night has passed and it's time to go back to work.

Love is powerful, effective, potent.

When we get our hearts fixed on something we earnestly desire, there is not much that can prevent us from pursuing that goal. It's something like a laser-guided missile when it is locked onto its target—there is little, if anything, that can stop it from reaching its objective.

With that picture in your mind, I want us to focus on wisdom today.

Tracking down wisdom is a key theme in the book of Proverbs. Wisdom is God's design for living and a reminder of Jesus Christ, whom the apostle Paul calls "the wisdom of God" and "in whom are hidden all the treasures of wisdom and knowledge" (1 Corinthians 1:24; Colossians 2:3).

Wisdom isn't something that's hidden in some secret place that we have to struggle to find. In fact, she calls out loud to us.

Wisdom calls aloud in the street, she raises her voice in the public squares. ~PROVERBS 1:20

We don't have go too far before we see that the wisdom of the world really isn't wisdom at all. We see people working themselves almost to death chasing after dreams of making it big someday. We see people pouring their last dollars into that lucky lotto ticket or dumping entire paycheques at the casino week after week with the same result: more losses. The world's systems are based on the world's insight and knowledge. These systems are faulty because they are not built on the firm foundation of Jesus Christ (2 Timothy 2:19).

Unbelievers have no fear of the Lord: they don't really care what his Word says and they don't apply God's principles and commands, thus treating their Creator like trash. They have no fear, no obedience, no reverence for God and his ways. With that attitude they cannot see or receive or even operate in wisdom because they don't fear him.

The fear of the Lord is the beginning of knowledge, but fools despise wisdom and discipline. ~PROVERBS 1:7

Before you fire a laser-guided missile, you need to have an objective, something to aim at so that you know if you hit the mark or not. Wisdom also requires you to know what you're going after.

Get skillful and godly Wisdom, get understanding (discernment, comprehension, and interpretation); do not forget and do not turn back from the words of my mouth.
~PROVERBS 4:5 AMP

The reverent and worshipful fear of the Lord is the beginning (the chief and choice part) of Wisdom, and the knowledge of the Holy One is insight and understanding.
~PROVERBS 9:10 AMP

Take a look at these facts about wisdom from the book of Proverbs. They will give you a better understanding of what wisdom is.

- *In her right hand is long life; in her left hand are riches and honour. (3:16)*

- *If you don't forsake Wisdom, she will protect you. (4:6)*

- *If you love wisdom, she will watch over you. (4:6)*

- *Esteem (value, respect, think highly of) wisdom and she will exalt (inspire, thrill, exalt) you. (4:8)*

- *We are to call wisdom our sister. (7:4)*

- *She is roommates with prudence. (8:12)*

- *She has possession of knowledge and discretion. (8:12)*

- *She hates pride and arrogance, evil behaviour and perverse speech.(8:13)*

- *Her walk is righteousness and she stays on the paths of justice. (8:20)*

- *She gives wealth to those who love her, making their accounts full. (8:21)*

- *If you find her you find life and get favour from the Lord. (8:35)*

- *If you don't find her, you harm yourself. (8:36)*

- *If you hate her, you love death. (8:36)*

The beginning of Wisdom is: get Wisdom (skillful and godly Wisdom)! [For skillful and godly Wisdom is the principal thing.] And with all you have gotten, get understanding (discernment, comprehension, and interpretation). ~PROVERBS 4:7 AMP

When we want something of this world, it pretty much doesn't matter what we have to do—we apply ourselves and go after it. We put in overtime, sacrificing sleep and even food just to get what we desire. If we know that God's wisdom is supreme and we need that wisdom, then why not go after wisdom in the same way we go after things of this world, which aren't going to last?

I am speaking in familiar human terms because of your natural limitations. For as you yielded your bodily members [and faculties] as servants to impurity and ever increasing lawlessness, so now yield your bodily members [and faculties] once for all as servants to righteousness (right being and doing) [which leads] to sanctification. ~ROMANS 6:19 AMP

Get into the Word; get books, teaching discs and DVDs. There is a wealth of knowledge to be taken in and there are many good men and women of God handling the Word correctly that would benefit you incredibly if you'd take the time to get understanding from the materials that they are putting out. Go after wisdom and understanding the way you used to go after things that netted you little.

Say to wisdom, "You are my sister," and call
understanding your kinsman. ~PROVERBS 7:4

Do this daily. Just say, "Wisdom you are my sister and understanding my kinsman." Speak it out and call it in. Go after wisdom and don't allow anything to trip you up or slow you down.

So shall you know skillful and godly Wisdom to be thus
to your life; if you find it, then shall there be a future and
a reward, and your hope and expectation shall not be cut
off. ~PROVERBS 24:14 AMP

What is the opposite of wisdom? Foolishness.

So how do you know if you're on Wisdom's side or on the foolish losing team?

It's how you handle God's Word.
How you obey his Word.
How you apply it.
And how you use it.

What do I mean by that?

For the story and message of the cross is sheer absurdity
and folly to those who are perishing and on their way to
perdition, but to us who are being saved it is the
[manifestation of] the power of God. ~1 CORINTHIANS 1:18 AMP

Is God's Word foolishness to you? Just answering that question with a "No" really doesn't answer the question. Your actions and your lifestyle make the verdict loud and clear.

As a born again, Bible-confessing, blood-bought, Holy Spirit-filled child of the Most High God, you are righteous in his sight. You were never designed to lose or remain at the bottom. God's Word says we are the head and not the tail; we're above and not below.

And that's just the start! Get into the Word and know who you are. Wisdom will lead you if you let her.

"My" God

Fear not [there is nothing to fear], for I am with you; do not look around you in terror and be dismayed, for I am your God. I will strengthen and harden you to difficulties, yes, I will help you; yes, I will hold you up and retain you with My [victorious] right hand of rightness and justice.
~ISAIAH 41:10 AMP

A t one time or another most of us have been gripped by fear. We have been afraid that things that happened in the past can hurt us in the present.

Afraid of what people think.
Of what people would do.
We have been afraid of the future.
Afraid of circumstances.
Afraid of ourselves.

One of the disguises that fear wears is the mask of worry. When we keep on worrying, we make life miserable for ourselves and for those who have to listen to us!

I tell you, My friends, do not dread and be afraid of those who kill the body and after that have nothing more that they can do. But I will warn you whom you should fear:

*fear Him Who, after killing, has power to hurl into hell
(Gehenna); yes, I say to you, fear Him! ~LUKE 12:4–5 AMP*

We fear God when we trust Jesus to save us from sin
(Isaiah 53:5–6, Romans 5:1), and when we fear God we
don't have to fear anything or anybody. God is originally
speaking to Israel here in our opening verse, but I believe
that this verse is applicable to all born again Christians.
God tells us not to fear. This is a command. When we fear
things God tells us not to fear we are disobeying God!

What I like about Isaiah 41:10 is that we are told why
we shouldn't fear, and these reasons are centred on God! In
telling us not to fear, Isaiah is telling us something about
God. Actually, he tells us five things about God that should
help keep us from living in fear and worry:

- *My GOD IS HERE* – "Fear not [there is nothing to
  fear], for I am with you." *(see also Psalm 18:2.)*

- *My GOD IS UNIQUE* – "Do not look around you in
  terror and be dismayed, for I am your God."

- *My GOD IS SOLID* – "I will strengthen and harden
  you to difficulties."

- *My GOD IS REALISTIC* – "Yes, I will help you."

- *My GOD IS ENDLESS* – "Yes, I will hold you up and
  retain you with My [victorious] right hand of
  rightness and justice."

When fear comes around, turning quickly into worry,
we need to stop and take a look at our God. You see, the
whole point of hiding God's Word in our hearts (Psalm
119:11) is so the Holy Spirit has something to work with
when fearful situations come around (John 14:26). When

we have God's Word firmly planted in us and don't doubt it, Jesus says this,

> *And Jesus answered them, Truly I say to you, if you have faith (a firm relying trust) and do not doubt, you will not only do what has been done to the fig tree, but even if you say to this mountain, Be taken up and cast into the sea, it will be done.* ~MATTHEW 21:21 AMP

Having an abundance of God's Word stored up in your heart—not just in your memory but in your reality (Luke 6:45)—when storms come allows you to respond without fear and worry, because when fear comes knocking, you send faith to answer it. Do you know what happens when you do that?

> *So be subject to God. Resist the devil [stand firm against him], and he will flee from you.* ~JAMES 4:7 AMP

Fear has nothing in common with you. You have been given a Spirit of power and of love and a sound mind (2 Timothy 1:7 KJV).

Prosper

prosper | präspər |
• flourish physically; grow strong and healthy[3]

Everybody wants to prosper. Who wants to stay the same, thinking the same thoughts as last week, or a month or a year ago? Who would want to remain in the first grade for the rest of their lives? To live in time is to change. Without change you will never prosper.

In order for our bodies to prosper we have to give them rest, exercise, wholesome food, clean water and other beneficial tools. For our Spirits to prosper we need to feed them as well. The Word of God is the food that causes our souls to prosper. As with our bodies, however, it's not just a matter of taking in nourishment and sitting around idle— God's Word needs application to see its full effect. Our walk with Jesus has to keep growing; it cannot stay the same.

God's promises are new every morning (Lamentations 3:23). His blessings, his grace and his mercy are new every day. Why try to live on yesterday's hopes, dreams and

---

[3] *New Oxford American Dictionary, 2nd Edition* (New York: Oxford University Press, 2005). s.v. prosper.

blessings when each day God has bigger and better things for you?

I want to show you how to prosper, so I am going to give you a few pointers so you can understand how to thrive in your relationship with Jesus and walk in all the fullness he came to give (Colossians 2:10).

> *So then, just as you received Christ Jesus as Lord,*
> *continue to live in him, rooted and built up in him,*
> *strengthened in the faith as you were taught, and*
> *overflowing with thankfulness. See to it that no one takes*
> *you captive through hollow and deceptive philosophy,*
> *which depends on human tradition and the basic*
> *principles of this world rather than on Christ. ~COLOSSIANS 2:6-8*

1. Stay on target. (v. 6)

You received Jesus into your heart by faith. You were dead in your sins and destined to hell when you prayed a prayer asking Jesus into your heart to forgive you of all of your sins. In that one simple prayer you trusted God to hear you and clear you because of Jesus' sacrifice. That took faith.

> *So then just as you received Christ Jesus as Lord . . .*

You started your walk with faith, now keep on target. (Also see 2 Corinthians 4:18.)

2. Be consistent. (v. 7)

> *. . . rooted and built up in him, strengthened in the faith*
> *as you were taught, and overflowing with thankfulness.*

We need to get our roots deep into God's Word. Trees that make it through wind storms and drought seasons have grown their roots down into the earth, where they are not only anchored but also tapped into enough water to sustain them. We need to have the roots of our faith and hope deep in God's Word, where there is an abundant supply of living water.

3. Keep your eyes open. (v. 8)

See to it that no one takes you captive through hollow and deceptive philosophy, which depends on human tradition and the basic principles of this world rather than on Christ." (Also see 1 Timothy 4:1)

There are many false teachers in our world teaching ideas that have a hint of truth to them but are not based on the Word of God. We need to be on guard so we don't get fooled by these people. If what is being said is not what God's Word says, then walk away. Our salvation is not built on how good we are, how well we treat other people or even on how much money we give. These are all good things to do, and we should do them, but our righteousness is built on Jesus Christ and his finished work on the cross.

When you become intimately acquainted with God's Word, if someone attempts to deceive you with what they say you should do as a born again believer based on human traditions to gain favour with God, you will recognize it as a lie immediately. Anybody telling you that your salvation depends on your good works is not telling you the truth.

To prosper we need to check our food source. Are we filling up on God's Word every day? Does what we listen to line up with the Word of God?

- *To prosper we need to stay on our faith walk. (Psalm 119:11)*

- *To prosper we need to stay rooted in the Word. (Mark 4:20–22)*

- *To prosper we need to be careful of what we let into our hearts. (Proverbs 4:23)*

- *To prosper we need to serve our local church and become a vital part of that community. (Hebrews 10:24–25)*

God's Word is seed and the seed will do exactly what it was sent for (Isaiah 55:11), so keep sowing it in your life and in the lives of others. Grow the spiritual bumper crop that you were intended to grow.

Everything that is alive is growing. Without life there is no growth; without growth there is no life. Prosperity is God's idea. Everything finds its beginning and end in him. To prosper in every area of life is to live every day for Jesus, allowing his life to shine through us to those who do not yet know him.

"For I know the plans I have for you," declares the LORD, "plans to prosper you and not to harm you, plans to give you hope and a future." ~JEREMIAH 29:11

Re-run

O n the "Life Network" on my cable TV package I recently watched a family bring their teenage daughter to a hospital for brain surgery. They all looked pretty stressed out, especially (understandably) the girl's mother.

A week later, I turned on my TV only to see a "re-run" of the same family bringing in the same daughter for the same surgery. This time, however, I found myself saying, "Hey, mother, don't worry; I saw the outcome last week and all is well. I saw the end of the show—she wins! So trust me, relax, all is well!" Of course, the mother couldn't hear me, but if she could have, I wonder if she would have listened and just relaxed as the scenario played out?

Jesus has already been to the end of time. He was there at the beginning, when the world and everything in it was being put together (Genesis 1), and he has been at the end (Revelation 22:13).

Jesus knows what's coming next for you. He has a plan.

When you were being put together inside your mother's womb, Jesus knew you. He knew what your name would be, where you were going to live and what you were going to do. He knows you right now; he knows that you're reading this book and knows how it's going to benefit you (Psalm 139:16).

God has a destiny planned for you and he knows what's best for you. Now all you have to do is obey. When you asked Jesus into your life, he gave his Holy Spirit to live in you (2 Corinthians 1:22), to guide you and teach you and to remind you of what you've read and heard in his Word (John14:26). Learn to listen for God's leading by being obedient to his Word. Don't question with "ifs, ands or buts"—just do it.

God and his Word are completely trustworthy. His plan is to prosper you, not to harm you (Jeremiah 29:11), and not only that—you can spread the Good News about Jesus Christ to the hurting, the dying and the lost so that they, too, can give God praise, glory and honour.

Like I wanted to reassure the mother on TV, so God is telling us in his Word and by his Holy Spirit, "Trust me, it's all good!"

No weapon formed against you will prevail. ~ISAIAH 54:17

There are going to be rough times—some of them really tough—but if we continue to stay focused on Jesus and his Word, none of those situations will destroy us, for Jesus has overcome the world and all that goes with it (John 16:33). We're all going to stumble and make mistakes (James 3:2); however, even failure cannot keep us defeated. It remains our choice: we can choose to stay down or we can rise above the situation, using it as a stepping stone (Proverbs 24:16).

I have read the end of the book . . . we win! We are "playing" in a "game" that has already been won! We are living a life that has already been determined; the outcome is sure.

As a born again believer, don't worry about what's going on around you (Matthew 6:25); live your life to the full the way God intended you to live it (John 10:10b). God has called you, chosen you, bought and paid for you. He's got a hold of you (See Isaiah 41:9–13), so don't worry (this isn't a suggestion, it's a command). You are on the winning team! You are a winner!

But even better, you are an ambassador for Christ on this planet! We are Christ's representatives. From God's perspective, our time on this earth is something like a re-run: he knows the end; he's got the script. He knows those who will choose to be faithful and get the victor's crown.

Stop here for a minute: How do you think you should live for Jesus knowing this?

- *Act like the WINNER you are!*

- *Act like the CHOSEN OF GOD that you are!*

- *Act like the REDEEMED PERSON Almighty God says you are!*

Therefore, since we are surrounded by such a great cloud of witnesses, let us throw off everything that hinders and the sin that so easily entangles, and let us run with perseverance the race marked out for us.
~HEBREWS 12:1

You are blessed to be a blessing. Now walk in that!

Smashing "Stinking Thinking"

Have you ever felt like the whole world was against you or that your life was about to drop into a bottomless pit? You're not alone. Many people have had those exact feelings, and some may even be experiencing them right now.

Sometimes it feels like we are solitary figures—that everybody is out to get us and those we once trusted are against us. Sometimes we feel like we are worth very little to anybody and assume that others have much more to offer than we do. These feelings and thoughts are what I call "stinking thinking." If you are a Christian, then consider the following three keys very seriously, for they are the very steps that will help you smash "stinking thinking" in your life.

1) See yourself the way God sees you.

The Word refers to us all when it notes, *"As he thinks in his heart, so is he"* (Proverbs 23:7a AMP). If we focus on how weak or limited our abilities are, that is exactly what we will become. If we think we can't do something, we can't—or at least we'll never try because we've already convinced ourselves that there's no use in trying because we can't do it. If you don't see yourself as a child of God, a redeemed, forgiven new creation, then you most certainly will not act that way.

The Bible indicates that as we think in our hearts so we are. How do we see ourselves?

We were created in the image of Christ and God values each one of us as his creation.

His divine power has given us everything we need for life and godliness through our knowledge of him who called us by his own glory and goodness. ~2 PETER 1:3

God has given us everything we need for living a life pleasing to him. This comes through knowing him, which comes through knowing his Word. When we spend time reading the Bible and thinking about what we've read, we begin to see who God proclaims we are and what he says we can do.

We can do all things through Christ who strengthens us (Philippians 4:13).

The Holy Spirit is with us to guide us into truth, to remind us of what we've heard and read in the Word (John 14:26).

The same Holy Spirit that raised Lazarus from the dead is the same Holy Spirit you received when you gave your life to Jesus (2 Corinthians 1:21). The same Holy Sprit that called Jesus out of the tomb and raised him from the dead is one and the same Holy Spirit that I have living in me and you have living in you if we're living for Jesus.

2) Speak your faith and not your fear.

Many of us can talk ourselves right out of God's best for our lives. It's true—we can't live victoriously if we refuse to get a grip on our words.

Jesus said we will have whatever we say (Mark 11:23). This can work in either the negative or the positive, depending on what we are saying. For example, I've talked to many people who said they'd never be able to quit smoking, and they were right! They kept speaking their fear rather than declaring faith in Jesus, the One who gives the gift of self-control.

We say "I can't" so often that we coach ourselves into believing that we can't, which leaves us feeling useless and weak. Then we end up on the train of "stinking thinking" with a one-way ticket in our pocket, heading full blast down the tracks away from the plans God has for our lives.

The tongue has the power of life and death, and those who love it will eat its fruit. ~PROVERBS 18:21

If you don't like what you have right now, take a minute to remember what you have been saying about it. Look at the things your mouth has been confessing. When we mix our confession with faith, the power of God goes into operation and that power is released into the situation we are facing and fills it with God's ability. We will have whatever we say.

Speak faith, not fear. God has called you out of the old system of death, so affirm the new life he has called you to. Don't continually go back to the old ways—speak your faith.

Fear not, for I have redeemed you; I have summoned you by name; you are mine. ~ISAIAH 43:1B

Speak your faith, not your fears!

3) Focus on the promise, not the problem.

Let us fix our eyes on Jesus, the author and perfecter of our faith, who for the joy set before him endured the cross, scorning its shame, and sat down at the right hand of the throne of God. Consider him who endured such opposition from sinful men, so that you will not grow weary and lose heart. ~HEBREWS 12:2

Merry-go-rounds are nice enough at amusement parks, but in terms of our thought patterns, focusing on the problems and not the promises will take us as far forward as a carousel horse that never leaves its circular track. We can't solve problems by using the same kind of thinking we used to get ourselves into the mess—that's insanity! How can we keep doing the same things and yet expect a different outcome?

We have to turn our focus in a different direction. We must focus on the promise! Let us fix our eyes on Jesus, the author and perfecter of our faith.

When the enemy tells us we aren't able to get to where we are going, we need to let him know that God has put a "but" in that sentence; our sufficiency is from God.

Jesus didn't say only some things are possible; he said with God all things are possible (Matthew 19:26). It doesn't matter what you're struggling with—cigarettes, booze, drugs, an eating disorder, depression, thoughts of suicide, feelings of hopelessness—God is bigger than all of them put together. When you keep your eyes on Jesus and his promises, you will see yourself the way God sees you. When that happens there is just simply no room for "stinking thinking" in your life!

Focus on the promise, not the problem.

Are you sick and tired of being sick and tired?

Are you ready to move on with God?

Are you willing to trust God and be the person he has called you to be?

Then start talking the talk and walking the walk!

Worry, fear and feelings of being weak and hopeless are all to be left behind us. We are chosen of God, cleansed by the blood of Jesus Christ, and we have been given the Holy Spirit. We are the righteousness of God (1 Corinthians 1:30).

Now stand up, Saint. Be who you are!

This is the day the Lord has made; let us rejoice and be glad in it. ~PSALM 118:24

Staying Green

Staying green has nothing to do with jealousy, nor am I referring to lifestyle choices that protect the natural world around us. Today I want us to think about staying fresh, alive, producing life even when it seems to be avoiding you.

I have experienced days, weeks and even months when life has seemed hopeless, numb and empty. I'm glad to say those are things of the past. When it seems like the lights of life are turned out (or at least dimmed to near darkness), I've learned what to do and what not to do.

1. Don't turn back to your old ways *(Galatians 5:1; Ephesians 6:14; 2 Thessalonians. 2:15).*

If you've ever stumbled in your walk with Jesus, you know firsthand how the enemy likes to lure us with things that look good and right. Then, after the bait is taken and the hook set, the horrible feelings of failure and defeat pour in like a tsunami wave.

When you are faced with tough times, don't turn back from confessing God's Word. Never allow circumstances to dictate how you feel or how you see God or his Word. What you see going on around you does not change the truth about God's Word; rather, God's Word changes what's going on in your life. It is God's Word that will bring you though and sustain you.

> *Your Word is a lamp to my feet and a light to my path.*
> ~PSALM 119:105

> *For I the Lord your God hold your right hand; I am the Lord, Who says to you, Fear not; I will help you!* ~ISAIAH 41:13 AMP

> *The name of the Lord is a strong tower; the [consistently] righteous man [upright and in right standing with God] runs into it and is safe, high [above evil] and strong.*
> ~PROVERBS 18:10 AMP

The writer of Hebrews puts it this way:

> *For the Word that God speaks is alive and full of power [making it active, operative, energizing, and effective]; it is sharper than any two-edged sword, penetrating to the dividing line of the breath of life (soul) and [the immortal] spirit, and of joints and marrow [of the deepest parts of our nature], exposing and sifting and analyzing and judging the very thoughts and purposes of the heart.*
> ~HEBREWS 4:12 AMP

The enemy comes to steal from you, to kill and to destroy (John 10:10a). He will try to make things look worse than they are and show you only the dark side. He will try to blind your eyes, your thoughts and your heart from God's Word because he knows it is the light of truth that destroys darkness, making him run in terror (James 4:7; Ephesians 6:13).

The enemy will try to get you feeling sorry for yourself, like you're in this alone with no way out and no one who cares. These are all very cheap tricks, but if you fall for them they become powerful weapons against you.

So what are we to do?

Don't turn back, but continue moving forward with God. You trusted him and his Word when you asked Jesus into your heart and life to forgive you and cleanse you. Now continue to trust him. If God is God of your life when all is well and the sun is shining in your life, then he remains the same God even when you feel the bottom has dropped out. God and his Word never change (James 1:17; Hebrews 13:8).

So don't be fooled into "jumping ship" just because the waves are getting a little wild. Keep to the path, continuing to trust God and his Word (Proverbs 3:5–6; Hebrews 12:2).

2. Stay Green

[Most] blessed is the man who believes in, trusts in, and relies on the Lord, and whose hope and confidence the Lord is. ~JEREMIAH 17:7 AMP

- *God has a plan for your life. (Jeremiah 29:11)*

- *God laid out a plan for your life and wrote it down in his book. (Psalm 139:16)*

- *Trust God! Believe him when he says, "Never will I leave you." (Hebrews 13:5)*

Verse 8 of Jeremiah 17 goes on to say,

For he shall be like a tree planted by the waters that spreads out its roots by the river; and it shall not see and fear when heat comes; but its leaf shall be green. It shall not be anxious and full of care in the year of drought, nor shall it cease yielding fruit.

Trees that grow next to the river don't worry about whether the rains come or not. They have a steady supply of water. Their roots have gone down to the river, which supplies them with all the water they need. These trees don't panic in hard times; even when a drought comes their leaves stay fresh and green. When other plants farther away from the stream are withering and dying, they are producing fruit—all because they are planted next to the water source.

"Staying green" applies to hard times. If you are planted in the Word of God, drinking up its goodness, when the drought does come you can continue to take in life from your Source, producing fruit the way you were designed to (Galatians 5:22–23).

Droughts and storms never come to make us stronger; they come to test our "root system," to test the foundation we have built on. When we drink in God's Word on a daily basis we need not fear those tests.

A thousand may fall at your side, and ten thousand at your right hand, but it shall not come near you.
~PSALM 91:7 AMP

Focus on the promise, not the problem. Stay Green!

Step Up and Step Out

Today I challenge you to be a disciple of Jesus Christ! Step out and step it up—live today like you really are who you say you are.

And He said to all, If any person wills to come after Me, let him deny himself [disown himself, forget, lose sight of himself and his own interests, refuse and give up himself] and take up his cross daily and follow Me [cleave steadfastly to Me, conform wholly to My example in living and, if need be, in dying also]. ~LUKE 9:23 AMP

To become a disciple, you first need Jesus Christ to be your Lord and Saviour (See John 3:1–18). Next, Jesus tells us what is involved in true discipleship.

1. Make up your mind.

This is not just a decision that you make today because the mood is right and the Holy Spirit is calling—tomorrow you will need to give it much more than lip service. When you say yes to Jesus, it's a decision that needs to be taken very seriously because it will cost you.

Yet to all who received him, to those who believed in his name, he gave the right to become children of God.
~JOHN 1:12

This means we are not our own; we are his, so we don't have the right to complain when God calls us to do a certain task or take on a certain position.

Does the ax raise itself above him who swings it, or the saw boast against him who uses it? As if a rod were to wield him who lifts it up, or a club brandish him who is not wood! ~ISAIAH 10:15

When we say yes to Jesus, we make up our mind to respond in this way: "Lord, you are in control. I will go with whatever you call me to."

2. Chart your course.

When we say yes to Jesus, we turn from our own ways, turn our care over to him and follow him completely in faith, knowing he is our all in all. We call that repentance, which means to go in the opposite direction to where we were heading in when we were in control of our lives. We chart a new course with God's guidance (Psalm 119:101–106).

3. Learn to say no.

There are many things that call out for our attention when we have decided to spend some time with the Lord. We think about the TV or the movie that's just been released or toy with the idea of calling up some friends to go out. Instead, we need to learn how and when to say No when watching a show or just sitting around seems more inviting than praying or reading God's Word. We need to say no to the thoughts that so regularly parade through our minds.

We demolish arguments and every pretension that sets itself up against the knowledge of God, and we take captive every thought to make it obedient to Christ.
~2 CORINTHIANS 10:5

Discipleship is about saying no to the things that lure us away from God's best in many areas of our lives.

4. Forget about yourself.

I have been crucified with Christ and I no longer live, but Christ lives in me. The life I live in the body, I live by faith in the Son of God, who loved me and gave himself for me. ~GALATIANS 2:20

We are dead to this world but alive because of Jesus. This is not our home; we are aliens and strangers on this planet and this is just a layover until we get home (Ephesians 2:19; Hebrews 11:13). We are not just humans having a spiritual experience, we are spiritual beings having a human experience (Romans 6:11; 8:10).

Forgetting about yourself or "taking up your cross" means dying to your desires daily, putting off your plans and taking up the will of God (Luke 9:23).

Going after God's will for every situation is more about a lifestyle of following Jesus than having strings to pull during an uncertain moment. It means not turning and walking away when things don't go your way, choosing instead to reach out, speak out and stand out in Jesus' name. That moment may very well be the time God is preparing to make his way known to you.

Pray continually. ~1 THESSALONIANS 5:17

We keep our focus on Jesus by staying in communication with him. The verses that follow in 1 Thessalonians 5 show us how:

. . . give thanks in all circumstances . . . ~v. 18

Why?

. . . for this is God's will for you in Christ Jesus. ~v. 18

Being a dedicated follower of Jesus will help us to not put out the Spirit's fire (v. 19) or treat prophecies with contempt (v. 20) but to test everything and hold on to the good (v.21). Our dedication will help us avoid every kind of evil (v. 22).

Then verse 23 closes off with a blessing:

May God himself, the God of peace, sanctify you through and through. May your whole spirit, soul and body be kept blameless at the coming of our Lord Jesus Christ.

We've been given power and authority to do the works of Jesus Christ on this planet right now. (Matthew 28:18–20)

For as many as are the promises of God, they all find their Yes [answer] in Him [Christ]. For this reason we also utter the Amen (so be it) to God through Him [in His Person and by His agency] to the glory of God. But it is God Who confirms and makes us steadfast and establishes us [in joint fellowship] with you in Christ, and has consecrated and anointed us [enduing us with the gifts of the Holy Spirit]; [He has also appropriated and acknowledged us as His by] putting His seal upon us and giving us His [Holy] Spirit in our hearts as the security deposit and guarantee [of the fulfillment of His promise]. ~2 CORINTHIANS 1:20–22 AMP

We are exactly who God says we are—so let's step up and step out and live in the power and the freedom and the victory that is ours in Christ!

Stir It Up!

That is why I would remind you to stir up (rekindle the embers of, fan the flame of, and keep burning) the [gracious] gift of God, [the inner fire] that is in you by means of the laying on of my hands [with those of the elders at your ordination]. For God did not give us a spirit of timidity (of cowardice, of craven and cringing and fawning fear), but [He has given us a spirit] of power and of love and of calm and well-balanced mind and discipline and self-control. ~2 TIMOTHY 1:6–7 AMP

I enjoy a good campfire: sitting around with friends, laughing, talking and the best part—sharing our hearts and our struggles with each other. And I'm not talking about just any group of people but the close people in our lives that are safe to share our hearts with. Times like that are good.

Sometimes it's painful, but we know that there are times when to truly be a friend you have to say the hard stuff as well (Proverbs 27:6). If we want to see others grow into what God has called them to be, we need to help them see the areas or attitudes in their lives that they can't see. In the same breath, we also need to be open to our friends' words to us. Encouraging words stir us up.

Like a campfire that burns brighter and gives off more heat when the embers take in more oxygen as it is stirred up, our walk with the Lord can also be fanned into flame by those around us. I was in a tough place and had a friend come along and share the Word of God with me (2 Timothy 2:15), reminding me of God's promises and encouraging me not to give up, not to give in. That stirring helped the flame of hope to burn bright again.

When we make juice crystals, iced tea, hot chocolate or instant coffee, the product needs to be stirred to bring out its best flavour. If we don't stir it up, the product settles and becomes of little use.

In the days of the gold rush, prospectors would sit beside the mountain streams, allowing the silt, sand and hopefully gold nuggets to drain into their pans. Then they would swirl the pans around, stirring up the water in order to sift out the gold. We are supposed to stir up one another and remind each other of the Word.

Sometimes in the daily struggles of life we can get so focused on what's in front of us that the distraction takes our eyes off Jesus. Other times we get settled where we are at. We feel life is good and we've got it made and we don't want to rock the boat so we just settle into our well-worn seat and maintain the status quo. Like Cool Aid or iced tea when they are not stirred up, our lives are tasteless or at best very weak. When we remind others of the Word of God, we remind ourselves too (Proverbs 11:25; 27:17).

Stirring up each other helps us to remember God's promises and focus on truth.

For God did not give us a spirit of timidity (of cowardice, of craven and cringing and fawning fear), but [He has given us a spirit] of power and of love and of calm and well-balanced mind and discipline and self-control.
~2 TIMOTHY 1:7 AMP

Stand on God's Word; encourage and stir up the power and authority that has been invested in you by Jesus Christ and as evidenced by the Holy Sprit in your life. Speak God's Word to yourself, your friends and the situations you are facing, Stir yourself up in the Word and then stir others up!

Remember, we are on the winning team! We are not defeated and cannot be defeated! Greater is Christ in you then any situation or problem you may face (Colossians 1:27; 1 John 4:4).

Now get going, Saint, and experience the joy of this new day!

That's Not My Name!

Have you ever heard the joke about the guy who goes to a football game? He's got a good seat, a big bag of peanuts and he's thrilled at the view he has of the entire field. Shortly into the game, he hears someone way up in the stands yell, "Hey Bill!" He sets down his peanuts, gets up and scans the upper deck from side to side, then shrugs his shoulders, shakes his head and sits back down. Before long, he hears it again: "Hey Bill!" and this goes on for some time. Finally, he gets tired of this name calling and gets up, turns around and yells into the crowd, "My name's not Bill!"

This story seems kind of unbelievable, and granted, it is; however, there are Christians today who still answer when the wrong name is called.

> *Therefore if any person is [ingrafted] in Christ (the Messiah) he is a new creation (a new creature altogether); the old [previous moral and spiritual condition] has passed away. Behold, the fresh and new has come!* ~2 CORINTHIANS 5:17 AMP

When you died to your old life by asking Jesus Christ into your heart, you became something that wasn't there before! Yes—the old you is gone! The old you is dead!

You know when someone leaves this earth that all that's left is the "earth suit" that was required for living life on this planet. (Just like people who have walked the moon needed a moon suit, we need an "earth suit" to walk this planet). Calling out the person's name when they are in the casket and heading for the gravesite helps nothing. They can't hear you. If you were to start cursing them and telling them how worthless they were, it wouldn't make any difference to them. They are dead to this world.

When you gave your life to Jesus, you entered into a blood covenant with him. Jesus took your name—"Sick," "Weak," "Loser," "Headed for Hell"—and gave you his name.

He took your place: he paid for your sins and gave you a new name with a new identity.

For our sake He made Christ [virtually] to be sin Who knew no sin, so that in and through Him we might become [endued with, viewed as being in, and examples of] the righteousness of God [what we ought to be, approved and acceptable and in right relationship with Him, by His goodness]. ~2 CORINTHIANS 5:21 AMP

God took the sin, the shame, the weakness, the sickness, the hopelessness, the failures—all of our sins—and dumped it on Jesus (1 Peter 2:24). He went to the cross to pay the price of sin (Romans 6:23). Because of that, now we are holy, righteous and new creations in God's sight.

Therefore, you are no longer a slave (bond servant) but a son; and if a son, then [it follows that you are] an heir by the aid of God, through Christ. ~GALATIANS 4:7 AMP; ALSO SEE EPHESIANS 2:19.

You have inherited a new name! You don't have to answer to "Loser" or respond to "you're never going to make it," "Hey Failure" or "Hey, you've blown it too many times to ever get back up" (Proverbs 24:16). Those names are not yours. They don't describe you and are not any part of you. The old you is gone—it's dead, now let it go. Your identity is in Jesus Christ.

Some people believe that God made the covenant with us. He didn't! God never made a covenant with us—God made the covenant with Jesus. If God made the covenant with each of us personally, it would be broken in the first few minutes of it being made because my guess is you and I have sinned at least once since we've asked Jesus into our hearts. Isn't that true?

If God made the covenant with us it would be over as soon as we sinned. Instead, the covenant was made with the perfect sacrifice, Jesus (Hebrews 10:14). And now, because we are in Christ (Colossians 1:27), we share in everything that belongs to Jesus (Romans 8:17).

God has given us his Holy Spirit to live in us (2 Corinthians 1:21–22) and we carry his name. In the Bible, Jesus is called:

Mighty God, Wisdom, Deliverer, Lion of the Tribe of Judah, Word of Life, Advocate, Provider, the Great I Am, Helper, Savior, Prince of Peace, Wonderful Counselor, Lamb of God, Lord of Hosts, Root of David, Author and Finisher of our Faith, the Way, Healer, Son of God, the Truth, Chief Cornerstone, King of Kings, Lord of Lords, Light of the World, Chief Shepherd, my Strength and Song, Righteous Judge, Son of

Righteousness, Resurrection and Life, the Alpha and Omega.

These names cover any need you'll ever have. The power of God is in his name to bring the attributes of his name to pass in your life (Acts 3:16).

Don't answer to names that aren't yours. When the enemy calls you down, turn off the volume. Ignore it— that's not you; it's not your name. Why on earth would you answer to it? It's like the guy at the football game; he was distracted from the game because he kept answering to a name that wasn't even his.

Come on, Saint, rise up! You are a child of the Most High God (John 1:12–13). You have been anointed (Isaiah 61:1; Luke 4:18). You have been chosen and called by name (Isaiah 41:9).

For we know that our old self was crucified with him so that the body of sin might be done away with, that we should no longer be slaves to sin—because anyone who has died has been freed from sin. Now if we died with Christ, we believe that we will also live with him. For we know that since Christ was raised from the dead, he cannot die again; death no longer has mastery over him. The death he died, he died to sin once for all; but the life he lives, he lives to God. In the same way, count yourselves dead to sin but alive to God in Christ Jesus. Therefore do not let sin reign in your mortal body so that you obey its evil desires. Do not offer the parts of your body to sin, as instruments of wickedness, but rather offer yourselves to God, as those who have been brought from death to life; and offer the parts of your body to him as instruments of righteousness. For sin shall not be your master, because you are not under law, but under grace.
~ROMANS 6:6–14

Know whose you are—act who you are.

You are blessed with every spiritual blessing! (Ephesians 1:3).

The Cross
Luke 23:32–43

We see the Cross on churches, jewellery, T-shirts and countless other items. Heavy metal bands use the cross on their album covers or wear them as big chunks of jewellery around their necks. It seems like the world wants to make the symbol of the cross just an ordinary thing, an everyday item that can be seen without understanding what it represents.

The cross is not a good luck charm. In the movies you see the actors holding up crosses to protect themselves from vampires and other dark forces. They think it has power to stop the devil. The fact remains that the cross was a tool, a death machine, a torture device, a one-way ticket to death. When people got nailed to a cross they were on their way to hours of horrible pain and a sure death, some enduring up to three days before they would breath their last breath.

What does the cross mean to you? The cross was only used for slaves and robbers and assassins and rebels. As a general rule, Roman citizens wouldn't be executed on a cross because it was too shameful of a way to die. For a Jew, the cross represented the worst way to die; it meant that you had been cursed by God.

> *Christ redeemed us from the curse of the law by becoming a curse for us, for it is written: "Cursed is everyone who is hung on a tree." ~GALATIANS 3:13*

Jesus was led out of the Jerusalem to be crucified, and two criminals were led out with him. When they came to a place called The Skull, the Roman soldiers crucified Jesus with one criminal on his left and one on his right. Here a prophecy came full circle: Isaiah had written hundreds of years before that Jesus would be numbered with the transgressors (Isaiah 53:12).

The crowds watching were mocking Jesus, and Luke tells us that even one of the criminals was slamming him: "Aren't you the Christ? Save yourself and us! If you're the Messiah, the Son of God, like you say you are, why don't You get out of this situation? And get us out of here too!" (Luke 23:39).

It's amazing how we see the same thing today. People are living in hopelessness and they still mock: "Jesus is the Son of God? I don't think so. Why doesn't he prove it? If he's God, why does he let disasters happen? Why this and why that?" People today mock the idea of Jesus being the Saviour of the world, just like that criminal hanging next to Jesus did.

The other criminal started to figure things out. Instead of keeping up with the cheap shots about Jesus, he got quiet and then confronted the other criminal:

> *"Don't you fear God," he said, "since you are under the same sentence? We are punished justly, for we are getting what our deeds deserve. But this man has done nothing wrong." ~LUKE 23:40B–41*

"We are getting what our deeds deserve." He defended Jesus, confessed his sin and then turned to Jesus and said, "Jesus, remember me, when you come into your kingdom." That's the same thing each one of us has to do when we choose to follow Jesus.

"O Lord, forgive me for my life of rebelling against you. Forgive me for mocking you by doubting and questioning you."

At that very moment Jesus was dying for all that man's criminal acts against society and against God. Jesus was paying for that. All the mockery? Jesus was paying for that too. What amazing love! Even as he suffered for this man, Jesus offered him forgiveness, an unconditional pardon and sure hope of eternal life.

Jesus does the same for us. All the different ways we have rebelled against God, all the moments of mocking and doubting God in our minds—right there on the cross, Jesus paid for those sins. Because of that moment on the cross, Jesus offers you an unconditional pardon, a clean slate and the sure hope of eternal life with him.

Jesus' words to the criminal are for us as well.

When we confess our sins and ask Jesus into our hearts, we get the assurance that we will be with Jesus in heaven when we die. We can also know that Jesus is with us as we face the events of this day.

You can be sure of your salvation. You can be sure God hears your prayers. You can be sure that you have eternal salvation because of the cross. Look at what God says in his Word:

God made him who had no sin to be sin for us, so that in him we might become the righteousness of God.
~2 CORINTHIANS 5:21

He himself bore our sins in his body on the tree, so that we might die to sins and live for righteousness; by his wounds you have been healed. ~1 PETER 2:24

Unlike the other high priests, he does not need to offer sacrifices day after day, first for his own sins, and then for the sins of the people. He sacrificed for their sins once for all when he offered himself. ~HEBREWS 7:27

He did not enter by means of the blood of goats and calves; but he entered the Most Holy Place once for all by his own blood, having obtained eternal redemption. ~HEBREWS 9:12

For Christ died for sins once for all, the righteous for the unrighteous, to bring you to God. He was put to death in the body but made alive by the Spirit. ~1 PETER 3:18

Good Friday is not something we should celebrate only one day out of the year; it should be a daily celebration, walking in the authority Jesus came to give.

For the message of the cross is foolishness to those who are perishing, but to us who are being saved it is the power of God. ~1 CORINTHIANS 1:18

What does the cross mean to you?

TW TT & TL

I just got in from a long, silent walk in one of the many amazing green spaces in our city. The day has been overcast and rainy for the most part. The park was quiet, the wind had stopped, the rain was on hold and all I could hear while I strolled through the bushy paths of the park were the birds, who seemed to be celebrating the amazing evening weather that the long wet day had left us with. It seemed almost surreal with the stillness and warmth and the relaxing smells of cedars and evergreens and wet earth, grass and wood. As my senses soaked in all that was going on around me, a verse came to mind:

> *Jesus said to him, I am the Way and the Truth and the Life; no one comes to the Father except by (through) Me.*
> ~*JOHN 14:6 AMP*

I think most people who call themselves Christ's followers know Jesus as the only way to eternal life (Acts 4:12). And I believe that most would also agree that Jesus is "the Truth." But how many of us really know Jesus as "the Life"?

Now before you go off at the mouth, stop for a second and think this through.

I was forced this evening to ask myself that question as well. Being surrounded by God's amazing creation, I had to make myself leave the business of the day and all the thoughts and things to remember and just become quiet within myself to enjoy the peace of God that filled every step I took. I was reminded again that God's peace isn't just in the quiet walk in the park; his peace is with me all day. It's just that sometimes I forget to stop and enjoy him (Psalm 119:165).

Jesus came to give us life to the full measure (John 10:10b). We are to have a continual party going on (Proverbs 15:15). That doesn't mean jumping around and shouting all the time, but when the day is full and long and heavy, we can celebrate that great peace of God that's tough to figure out (Philippians 4:7).

> *I have been crucified with Christ [in Him I have shared His crucifixion]; it is no longer I who live, but Christ (the Messiah) lives in me; and the life I now live in the body I live by faith in (by adherence to and reliance on and complete trust in) the Son of God, Who loved me and gave Himself up for me.* ~GALATIANS 2:20 AMP

If you're feeling dragged down and beat up by the day and the events in it, stop and think about the life Jesus came to give. All the encouragement, strength, peace and joy you need has already been set up for simple access. Mind you, God isn't going to force you to live in the fullness he has given you in Jesus. He has done everything already; now it's up to you to receive and celebrate that life.

Do you know Jesus as "the Life"?

When you were born, you came into this world crying while those around you were celebrating. You had left the only world you knew to enter into one you knew very little about. A time is coming when again you will leave a world that you know to go into another you know little about. Live your life in such a way that when you exit this planet through the door of death the world will cry and you will celebrate!

Jesus: the Way, the Truth, and the Life

Together ... with Jesus
Romans 6:1–11

I've had people tell me that they think that God is mad at them when they make mistakes. Some people feel that because they haven't felt the urge to read the Word and spend some time in prayer that God is angry with them. That's just simply not true!

When we stay away from time in the Word and prayer, we're the ones walking away from the relationship, not God. When we choose not to drink from the living water, God's Word, we are the ones who go thirsty. We are righteous in God's sight and we can't be under God's curse; Jesus took that curse for us and paid it in full (2 Corinthians 5:21).

We are not supposed to be looking at ourselves to see what disqualifies us from being united with Jesus; we are to look at and examine the fact that we are joined together with him (2 Corinthians 13:5). The following verses show us three ways in which we are united with Jesus:

In Death (Romans 6:1–3 AMP)

> WHAT SHALL we say [to all this]? Are we to remain in sin in order that God's grace (favor and mercy) may

multiply and overflow? Certainly not! How can we who died to sin live in it any longer? Are you ignorant of the fact that all of us who have been baptized into Christ Jesus were baptized into His death?

The price Jesus paid on the cross for our sins (Romans 5:8) isn't altered by our times of stumbling (James 3:2). The fact is Jesus went to the cross carrying our sins (1 Peter 2:24). If you have asked Jesus Christ into your heart to be your Lord and your Saviour and have been baptized, you are identified with Christ Jesus in his death. That old you is dead. Quit dragging that old you around—don't try CPR tactics to get it living again. Let it remain dead, along with all the memories that go with it. The old you was nailed to the cross with Jesus (Galatians 2:20).

In Resurrection (Romans 6: 4–6 AMP)

We were buried therefore with Him by the baptism into death, so that just as Christ was raised from the dead by the glorious [power] of the Father, so we too might [habitually] live and behave in newness of life. For if we have become one with Him by sharing a death like His, we shall also be [one with Him in sharing] His resurrection [by a new life lived for God]. We know that our old (unrenewed) self was nailed to the cross with Him in order that [our] body [which is the instrument] of sin might be made ineffective and inactive for evil, that we might no longer be the slaves of sin.

We are new creations in Christ (2 Corinthians 5:17). Something that wasn't there before we had Jesus in our hearts is there now that we are born again, baptized believers. God has given us his Holy Spirit as a deposit and to be our teacher that gives us life to the full.

[God has] set his seal of ownership on us, and put his Spirit in our hearts as a deposit, guaranteeing what is to come. ~2 CORINTHIANS 1:22

But the Comforter (Counselor, Helper, Intercessor, Advocate, Strengthener, Standby), the Holy Spirit, Whom the Father will send in My name [in My place, to represent Me and act on My behalf], He will teach you all things. And He will cause you to recall (will remind you of, bring to your remembrance) everything I have told you. ~JOHN 14:26 AMP

And if the Spirit of Him Who raised up Jesus from the dead dwells in you, [then] He Who raised up Christ Jesus from the dead will also restore to life your mortal (short-lived, perishable) bodies through His Spirit Who dwells in you. ~ROMANS 8:11 AMP

That curse no longer has any effect on us and has no permission to reside on or over us. We are free from the curse (Deuteronomy 28:15)—Jesus became that curse for us and overcame the curse by his resurrection (Galatians 3:13).

We used to be slaves to sin, weighed down with destructive systems and thoughts and actions. Now through Jesus we have no debt, duty, responsibility or obligation to that old nature. Many of those old ways demanded a lot of attention and energy, and we were willing to do whatever it took to maintain them. Now being new in Christ, we need to take at least that amount of energy to serve God by sharing the resurrected life with those around us. (Romans 6:19).

We are together with Jesus in his resurrection because we identified with his death in baptism.

We are together with Jesus . . .

In Freedom (Romans 6:7–11 AMP)

For when a man dies, he is freed (loosed, delivered) from [the power of] sin [among men]. Now if we have died with Christ, we believe that we shall also live with Him, Because we know that Christ (the Anointed One), being once raised from the dead, will never die again; death no longer has power over Him. For by the death He died, He died to sin [ending His relation to it] once for all; and the life that He lives, He is living to God [in unbroken fellowship with Him]. Even so consider yourselves also dead to sin and your relation to it broken, but alive to God [living in unbroken fellowship with Him] in Christ Jesus.

- *We are free in Christ.*

- *We don't have to live in the shadows of past failures.*

- *We don't have to listen to the lies of enemy.*

We believe that when we prayed the prayer of salvation we were instantly moved from the kingdom of darkness to the Kingdom of Light (Colossians 1:13). But sometimes the tougher part to realize is that we no longer have any obligation to sin. Our relationship with sin is done and we can live our lives fully in the freedom that Jesus has provided. Living free in Christ is living by faith—not responding to what our physical eyes see and ears hear but living and walking day to day by what the Word of God says (2 Corinthians 5:7).

What you believe about God (according to the Bible) is how he will be in your life. If you're not convinced that you can do all things through Christ (Philippians 4:13) and that you are more than a conqueror in Christ, then you are not going to step out in faith. Your belief will limit how you allow him to show his power in your life. However, if you do believe you are who God says you are, then you become an unstoppable force and a major pain to the devil and his plans.

You have been given power and authority to use Jesus' powerful, mighty name. You have been given freedom from hell, sin, Satan, death, sickness, disease and every other nasty thing that is listed in the curse. Jesus beat out the devil, and not by just a little bit—Jesus took the keys of death away from him (Revelation 1:18). Satan has no weapon great enough to overcome God or God's sons or daughters, but we have a weapon that overcomes the devil (Revelation 12:11).

Death holds no threat for the child of God. We are together with Jesus Christ. We are united with him (1 Thessalonians 5:9–11).

Stand up, Saint, and take your position. Pillage hell—populate heaven!

Truth

*Jesus said to those Jews who had believed in Him, If
you abide in My word [hold fast to My teachings and live
in accordance with them], you are truly My disciples. And
you will know the Truth, and the Truth will set you free.*
~JOHN 8:31–32 AMP

Without Jesus we are hopeless! We are sinners born into a sinful world. We are helpless and at the mercy of the devil. But when we give our hearts and lives to Jesus Christ by accepting his death on the cross and the resurrection and the life he brings, we come into a relationship with the Living God. We become co-heirs in the kingdom of God (Romans 8:17).

Now that we are new creations and have God's Holy Spirit living in us (2 Corinthians 1:22), Jesus commands us to continue doing what he did when he was living on this planet—to go after the lost.

*These twelve Jesus sent out with the following
instructions: "Do not go among the Gentiles or enter any
town of the Samaritans. Go rather to the lost sheep of
Israel. As you go, preach this message: 'The kingdom of
heaven is near.' Heal the sick, raise the dead, cleanse
those who have leprosy, drive out demons. Freely you
have received, freely give. Do not take along any gold or
silver or copper in your belts." ~MATTHEW 10:5–9*

Heal the sick who are there and tell them, "The kingdom of God is near you." ~LUKE 10:9

(Also see Luke 15 for three different stories about the joy of recovering that which was lost.)

When we do what Jesus did, we are "abiding" in (holding to, sticking with, continuing in) his Word (see John 8:31 above). We are partners in his mission, involved in a "co-mission." In Matthew 28, we see what our "co-mission" is:

Then Jesus came to them and said, "All authority in heaven and on earth has been given to me. Therefore go and make disciples of all nations, baptizing them in the name of the Father and of the Son and of the Holy Spirit, and teaching them to obey everything I have commanded you. And surely I am with you always, to the very end of the age." ~vv. 18–20

John 8:32 is a conditional promise. "If" we are not in God's Word—not applying it or doing what we have been commanded to—then verse 38 will be elusive to us. We won't know the truth; we won't have freedom. If we want to know the truth that sets us free, then we must go after that which Jesus came for: "The Lost."

Be the salt and light God has called you to be (Matthew 5:13–14).

Live such good lives among the pagans that, though they accuse you of doing wrong, they may see your good deeds and glorify God on the day he visits us.
~1 PETER 2:12

When we go after the lost and share God's love and God's powerful Word with them, we are obeying God, because he wants everyone to have eternal life (John 6:40). When we give of ourselves is when we are the most like Jesus (John 15:13).

Jesus gave everything for you. He gave up heaven to become a man. He was beaten, tortured and then killed by being nailed to a cross, three days later rising from the dead. All this was to prove that you are worth it (Romans 5:8). He came that you could have life to the full (John 10:10b).

> As the rain and the snow come down from heaven, and do not return to it without watering the earth and making it bud and flourish, so that it yields seed for the sower and bread for the eater, so is my word that goes out from my mouth: It will not return to me empty, but will accomplish what I desire and achieve the purpose for which I sent it. ~ISAIAH 55:10–11

Words are not just sounds. When God speaks things come into being. God cannot lie, so whatever he says becomes. We were created in his image. We were never intended to speak words that we didn't mean to come to pass. Speak God's Word over every situation—it will not return empty but will do exactly what he said it would.

Know truth—be free!

Wisdom

Wisdom is something we often hear about but seldom see put into action.

Our world is moving faster every day. Information travels at speeds that previous generations couldn't imagine. With this increase in speed, our lives can be forced into a frenzied pace, causing us to search for areas to trim time from. More often than not, that time is taken off our meal times or sleep times. Fast food on-the-go and burning the midnight oil in an attempt to capitalize on opportunities shows a lack of wisdom. If we are going to make it in the times ahead, wisdom has to be a discipline that we master.

Where does wisdom come from and how do we get it? James 1:5 tells us this:

> *If any of you lacks wisdom, he should ask God, who gives generously to all without finding fault, and it will be given to him.*

If you lack wisdom in your life, ask God. He is very willing to give it to you. Matthew 7:7–8 says this about asking God for what we need:

Ask and it will be given to you; seek and you will find; knock and the door will be opened to you. For everyone who asks receives; he who seeks finds; and to him who knocks, the door will be opened.

Today we are going to knock, seek and ask. Wisdom will be given to you if you go after it.

Let's start off by looking at the book of Proverbs.

Chapter one of Proverbs tells us what the book is all about (vv. 2-6):

For attaining wisdom and discipline; for understanding words or insight; for acquiring a disciplined and prudent life, doing what is right and just and fair; for giving prudence to the simple, knowledge and discretion to the young—let the wise listen and add to their learning, and let the discerning get guidance—for understanding proverbs and parables, the sayings and riddles of the wise.

This is how to benefit from wisdom:

My son, do not forget my teaching, but keep my commands in your heart, for they will prolong your life many years and bring you prosperity. ~PROVERBS 3:1–2

The first thing we are told is, "Do not forget . . . keep my commands in your heart."

We can hear a good message or even read a portion of Scripture that gives us new insight into something we previously didn't understand but then somewhere along the line forget what we heard or read. We may even forget the lesson the Holy Spirit revealed to us. That's what the writer of Proverbs is referring to here.

Do you want to have more life? Do you want all the years you should have to come to fulfillment? Then get God's Word not just into your head but into your heart. If you leave God's Word only in your head, you will soon start to use your own reasoning to override what you just learned. When the Word takes the elevator down from your head to your heart, stopping off at mouth level to confess it out loud, the Word becomes life and health to your whole body (Proverbs 4:22).

Do not forget what you have learned in and from the Word.

Let love and faithfulness never leave you; bind them
around your neck, write them on the tablet of your heart.
~PROVERBS 3:3

This can be a tough one. If it weren't possible to lose love and faithfulness, it would not have been mentioned. Therefore, we need to pay close attention, because love for God and the things of God, especially his people, can grow cold. *"Bind them around your neck, write them on the tablet of your heart."* We do this by reading the Word, confessing it and allowing it to flow through us daily.

Blessed are those who have learned to acclaim you,
who walk in the light of your presence, O Lord. They
rejoice in your name all day long; they exult in your
righteousness. For you are their glory and strength, and
by your favor you exalt our horn. ~PSALM 89:15–17

Because your love is better than life, my lips will glorify
you. I will praise you as long as I live, and in your name I
will lift up my hands. ~PSALM 63:3–4

Proverbs 3:4 goes on to tell us:

Then you will win favor and a good name in the sight of God and man.

When we focus on God's Word, it takes away self-centeredness, instead pointing us toward caring for what God cares for: his people. In serving others we are serving God. That is when we win the favour of both man and God.

Trust in the Lord with all your heart and lean not on your own understanding; in all your ways acknowledge him, and he will make your paths straight. Do not be wise in your own eyes; fear the Lord and shun evil. ~PROVERBS 3:5–7

Leaning on "our" understanding of what is going on around us leads to coming up with ideas for how to correct or, at the very least, avoid painful situations. But much of the time our understanding isn't pure. Our judgement of situations can be tainted by past experience and how we happen to be feeling in the moment, causing us to think we are seeing more clearly than we are.

There is good reason not to lean on our understanding but to trust the Lord to show us truth. The Word tells us that if we put our trust in the Lord, "*He will make our paths straight.*" It's not "He may"—the Word says, "He will!"

Do not be wise in your won eyes; fear the Lord and shun evil. This will bring health to your body and nourishment to your bones. ~PROVERBS 3:7–8

Think about this. When we trust the Lord and his Word, we attract health to our bodies (Proverbs 4:20–22; Isaiah 40:31)

Honor the Lord with your wealth and with the best part of everything you produce. Then he will fill your barns with grain, and your vats will overflow with good wine.
~PROVERBS 3:9–10 NLT

This is talking about tithing. Honouring God involves trusting him. Tithing is one of the ways we show our obedience and our trust in his faithfulness.

Tithing is about trust. People don't tithe because they don't trust God. They don't believe they will have enough to make it to the next payday if they give 10% to the work of God. In reality, those who tithe live better off the 90% they get to keep than those who try to make it on 100% of their income.

"Bring the whole tithe into the storehouse, that there may be food in my house. Test me in this," says the Lord Almighty, "and see if I will not throw open the floodgates of heaven and pour out so much blessing that you will not have room enough for it." ~MALACHI 3:10

God is saying, "Don't worry about the 10%; just give it to the work of the church and I'll look after you. Do you really think you can out-give me?"

If you haven't been tithing up until this point in your life, I encourage you to start. You are keeping the doors to miracle-working power closed in your life. Not tithing is not trusting, not obeying and not responding in faith.

Wisdom is what God wants in your life. With wisdom you don't need to stumble around wondering what you're here for, what God's will is for your life.

Proverbs 3:16 says about wisdom,

Long life is in her right hand; in her left hand are riches and honor.

Make a habit, starting today, to read one Proverb a day. There are 31 chapters in the book of Proverbs and many of our months have 31 days. On the months that don't have 31 days, simply double up your reading on a couple of days. Along with that, add one more habit that we are told about in Proverbs 7:4 . . .

Say to wisdom, "you are my sister," and call understanding your kinsman.

There is no need to stumble through life. God's Word will guide you. Get into the Word and allow the Word to get into you!

The Lord bless you and keep you in Jesus' name.

About the Author

Born and raised in Manitoba, Gord has dedicated his life to preaching and teaching God's Word for nearly twenty years. Encouraging God's people is a passion that consumes much of his time. Gord is a motivational speaker and life coach, speaking at camps, churches and other group events around the province.

To contact Gord, please email:
miyeinfo@gmail.com